A
PastorServe
RESOURCE

from Weakness to STRENGTH

8 Vulnerabilities That Can Bring Out
the Best in Your Leadership

Scott Sauls

foreword by Joni Eareckson Tada

David C Cook
transforming lives together

FROM WEAKNESS TO STRENGTH
Published by David C Cook
4050 Lee Vance Drive
Colorado Springs, CO 80918 U.S.A.

David C Cook U.K., Kingsway Communications
Eastbourne, East Sussex BN23 6NT, England

The graphic circle C logo is a registered trademark of David C Cook.

The website addresses recommended throughout this book are offered as a
resource to you. These websites are not intended in any way to be or imply an
endorsement on the part of David C Cook, nor do we vouch for their content.

Details in some stories have been changed to protect
the identities of the persons involved.

All Scripture quotations are taken from the ESV® Bible (The Holy Bible,
English Standard Version®), copyright © 2001 by Crossway, a publishing
ministry of Good News Publishers. Used by permission. All rights reserved.
The author has added italics to Scripture quotations for emphasis.

LCCN 2017934396
ISBN 978-0-7814-1313-8
eISBN 978-0-8307-7203-2

Published in association with the literary agency of Wolgemuth & Associates, Inc.

The Team: Tim Peterson, Amy Konyndyk, Nick Lee,
Jack Campbell, Susan Murdock
Cover Design: Jon Middel
Cover Photo: Getty Images

Printed in the United States of America
First Edition 2017

1 2 3 4 5 6 7 8 9 10

071417

Contents

Acknowledgments   5

Foreword: Before You Begin ...   9

Reflection   13

Introduction   19

Chapter 1   Ambition: The Catastrophe of Success   29

Chapter 2   Isolation: The Soil for Collapse   49

Chapter 3   Criticism: An Invitation to Self-Reflection   69

Chapter 4   Envy: A Thorn in the Soul   91

Chapter 5   Insecurity: Growing Big from Feeling Small   109

Chapter 6   Anticlimax: A Gateway to Hope   129

Chapter 7   Opposition: The Unlikely Pathway to Neighbor Love   149

Chapter 8   Suffering: Leading with a Limp   173

Epilogue   189

More about Scott Sauls   199

Notes   201

PastorServe Book Series   205

Acknowledgments

To Andrew and the team at Wolgemuth & Associates. Thank you for being the first to believe in me and for persisting in your effort in persuading me to become a writer of books. What once seemed silly to me has become a source of joy and another avenue for gospel ministry.

To Jimmy Dodd and David C Cook for asking me to do this project. Thank you for your generous investment in pastors and other leaders, including yours truly.

To Tim Keller. Your virtues have grown alongside, and continue even still to exceed, your influence. Knowing you first as a mentor, and now also as a friend, has led me to admire you even more for your prayerfulness, humility, and marriage than I do for your preaching—which, by the way, I still believe is the best in the world. Your private life and public life are a picture of the things I have written in these pages.

To Scotty Smith. From the earliest days of my ministry, you have been as a big brother *to* me, and always a champion *for* me. Your voice remains a steady echo of the Father's love, a welcome foreshadowing of his "Well done, good and faithful servant" that will be spoken over us all—not because we are great, but because Jesus envelops us into his greatness by grace alone. None has drilled this message into my heart like you have, dear friend. And you keep getting better—more humble, more kind, more wise, more childlike—with age.

To Gif, Anderson, Tom, Troy, Bill, Herbert, and Greg. Your lives mentor me. You are my friends. I'm thankful to be in the same cabin with each one of you.

To Bob Bradshaw. You are the secret weapon for the healthy, life-giving community that is Christ Presbyterian Church. You are a man who leads with impeccable character. I am thankful to lock arms with you and am proud to call you my friend.

To the pastors, staff, leaders, and congregation of Christ Presbyterian Church. You are family, and I love you.

To Joni. Your foreword to this book is of greater value than its chapters. Thank you for leading so well in the Luke 14 mandate to make the Father's house full. Thank you for showing us what it means, in real time, to live from weakness to strength.

To Abby and Ellie. God made you beautiful and special, and he loves you so much. And so does your dad. Don't ever forget that.

To Patti. Thank you for staying true to me and for being a source of strength when weakness has gotten the best of me by bringing out the worst in me. Thank you for pointing me to Jesus every single day—just by being you. Thank you for being the first and chief editor of every single page I have written since we started doing this—including this one. You are the secret coauthor who deserves a whole lot more credit than you receive. You are my best friend, the loyal and steady "6" to offset my always ambitious and sometimes impulsive "3," my partner and counselor and confidante, and the one I still want to grow old with. With you, there will never be such a thing as an empty nest. Life is always full with you in it.

To Mom. Though your memory is fading, your dignity and beauty are not. We are with you and for you always.

To Dad. The way you love and protect Mom makes me want to be a better man.

Before You Begin ...

If ever a book title described me, it's this one.

Years ago, when I took that fateful dive into shallow water and broke my neck, never did I think that God was honing me for leadership. All I could do was retch at the thought of sitting down for the rest of my life without use of my hands or legs. But slowly over time, God began opening doors and expanding my sphere of influence. I became a leader by default. And no one was more amazed than I.

Yet that's also the way things happen in the Bible. A Christian's suffering is always filled with surprise packages. God delights in handpicking people for leadership who are either stumbling bumblers *or* simply weak and ill equipped. It's what he did with Gideon. Right after God told Gideon that he was to go up against the

Midianites, God whittled his army down to a mere three hundred. Anyone will tell you, that's no way to win a war. Yet when Gideon crushed the Midianites, everyone knew that God had done it.

Sorry to disappoint you, world. It's just the way God enjoys getting things done. Consider how the Lord designed his gospel to go forth. When Jesus was ministering on earth, the twelve disciples—just common folk with ho-hum jobs—sort of half-believed in their Savior. The whole kingdom agenda looked like it was going nowhere.

Now, if I were God, I would do it differently. I'd pick the smartest men and women to be on my strategy team. I'd draft the world's sharpest millionaires to finance the operation. My public relations people would be the most effective communicators anywhere. Weak people need not apply. Those with physical defects? Forget it. People who might slow down my progress? Never.

Thank the Lord that I am not running the world. *He's* in charge. And he opens his arms to the weak and ungifted, the unlovely and unlikely. He opens his arms to sinners. It's because of his great love. It's also because this is the way God does things to bring maximum glory to himself.

My friend Scott Sauls has written an extraordinary book for people like me. *From Weakness to Strength* will force you to forget everything you've ever been taught about personal power leading to effective leadership. As a psychologist-friend once told me, confidence, charisma, and chutzpah count for little over the long haul. The leaders God chooses are often more broken than strong ... more damaged than whole ... more troubled than secure. God's greatest leaders do not rise up from a bed of roses; they rise from beds of nails.

It's why I thank God for my wheelchair—it is the bruising-of-a-blessing that has made me appreciate my failures and weaknesses. Never would I have dreamed I would serve God as an international disability advocate or an influential author. Never did I dream God would use me to influence the church or special-needs ministries. But it's the dream I am living. All because I have come to realize that God's most effective leaders don't rise to power *in spite of* their weakness; they lead with power *because* of their weakness.

I encourage you to read slowly and carefully the book you hold in your hands. It's filled with rich insights and sage wisdom. For Scott understands weakness. He resonates with people who have stumbled and fallen. And his friendship is one of my special joys of being in Christ's kingdom.

So, grab a cup of coffee and begin turning the pages of *From Weakness to Strength*—by the last chapter, you'll be shaking your head and thanking God for *your* bruised blessings, whether they be failures, botched surgeries, slowness of speech, long-standing losses, or maybe even a fateful dive into shallow water.

And may I say, from a fellow journeyman down the blood-stained road to Calvary, thank you for boasting in your weakness, delighting in the insults, and glorying in your suffering. It's the cast iron that makes you a ... *leader*.

Joni Eareckson Tada
Joni and Friends International Disability Center
Agoura Hills, California

Reflection

Scott Sauls's new book means more to me than it could possibly mean to most of you. That's not a boast, just an expression of affection for a dear brother with whom I've shared many seasons of leader-life over the course of our twenty-year friendship.

I am proud of Scott, but more so, I love him. I really want you to read this book, take it to heart, and buy copies for other leaders. And I want you to understand why it's not just another book on leadership.

Until leaders have suffered, and have learned to steward their pain, they don't really have much to offer. They may build a big platform and develop a cool "brand," but little else of lasting value.

I trust Scott to write this book, because for two decades I've had the honor of watching him increasingly boast in Christ, and in his own weaknesses. The longer I've known Scott, the more vulnerable he's become and, paradoxically, the more effective as a leader. And he's allowed me the privilege of walking with him during some of his most challenging seasons as a leader.

But I've also experienced Scott's willingness to enter the brokenness and vulnerability of other leaders as well—namely, me.

Scott first reached out to me when he was a young church planter in Kansas. I was a "seasoned" and, seemingly, successful church planter in Franklin, Tennessee. It didn't take me long to be drawn to Scott. When he first called, he didn't ask me for anything. He was simply intrigued with reports of what God was doing in our church family and wanted to encourage me.

Soon after our friendship began to grow, our Father took me into a painful season of breaking and healing—a season every leader will go through if they take the gospel seriously. God isn't nearly as concerned about what we're doing for Christ as he is committed to forming Christ inside us. God appointed a big fish to slow down and humble Jonah. He appointed a burnout for the same purpose in my life.

As a leader, I needed to discover the disparity between my outer success and my inner mess. I needed to own the disconnect between my head and my heart. I needed to grieve how much more alive and present I was in my pulpit than I was in my home. I needed healing for heart wounds I'd been carrying for forty years—wounds I denied and medicated poorly. Theoretical grace works well on theoretical brokenness, theoretical sins, and theoretical idols. My issues weren't theoretical.

Whatever illusions Scott may have had about me as a leader of a big, thriving church were short lived. But the truth is, Scott has never needed me to be impressive, smart, or sharp. He has always been just as comfortable with my struggles, weaknesses, and wounds as he has been affirming of my gifts. In fact, I don't remember Scott ever engaging me about pragmatic "shop talk" or ministry chops—as important as those matters are. Rather, he usually wants to talk about heart issues, relational matters, and the implications of the gospel.

Thank you, dear brother, friend, and partner in the gospel. May God increase your tribe.

Scotty Smith
Pastor, author, and teacher
The Gospel Coalition

"To keep me from becoming conceited because of the surpassing greatness of the revelations, a thorn was given me in the flesh, a messenger of Satan to harass me, to keep me from becoming conceited. Three times I pleaded with the Lord about this, that it should leave me. But he said to me, 'My grace is sufficient for you, for my power is made perfect in weakness.' Therefore I will boast all the more gladly of my weaknesses, so that the power of Christ may rest upon me. For the sake of Christ, then, I am content with weaknesses, insults, hardships, persecutions, and calamities. For when I am weak, then I am strong."

2 Corinthians 12:7–10

Introduction

If Jesus were with us in the flesh today, I wonder if we would accuse him of being un-American.

For as long as I can remember, I have loved being American. Yet I have often been caught in characteristically American trappings such as the pursuit of power, money, recognition, prestige, selfish ambition, making a name for myself, and advancing my interests, my agenda, my goals, my comfort, my privilege, and my view of the world.

As a young man, I took a trip to Jamaica with a few friends. Part of our visit included a brief stop in a Jamaican art gallery. As an American follower of Jesus, I was alarmed when I encountered a Jamaican painting of Jesus and his twelve disciples. To my surprise, all thirteen men in the painting (including Jesus) had brown skin, brown eyes, and black hair—betraying my long-held image of the white-skinned, blue-eyed, light-brown-haired,

English-speaking, American Jesus who could have easily passed as the fourth member of the Bee Gees. As I imagined him, Jesus was decidedly *American*. For this reason, my gut told me that something was off—perhaps even *wrong*—about the Jamaican portrayal.

Or, perhaps, the fault was not with the Jamaican artist. Perhaps the fault was with me.

Now, more than twenty years since that Jamaica visit, I have come to see that my home country is not and has never been at the center of the Christian story. Rather, we in America are members of the "ends of the earth" about whom Jesus spoke in the Great Commission of Matthew 28:16–20.

It turns out that the Jamaican image of Jesus was much truer to form than my culturally biased American one. The Jesus of Scripture is in all likelihood a brown-skinned, brown-eyed, black-haired, first-century Middle Eastern Jewish rabbi who never married, was materially poor, experienced homelessness, was more homely than handsome, never spoke a word of English, and never stepped foot on American soil.

Realizing these things does not take me to a place of shame. Rather, it takes me to a place of deep awe, gratitude, and worship. Through the corridors of time, from the other side of the world, and across language and ethnic and cultural and religious and economic barriers, this same Jesus purposed to include people like me—*Americans* like me—in his great story of redemption. Though Jesus is in many ways *un*-American, he is by no means *anti*-American. He is for people like me just as he was for his own contemporaries. Through sheer grace and based on nothing that I have contributed, he has grafted me into his everlasting family, which, although it is *first* for the Jew and *then* for the Gentile (Romans 1:16), is no less for me than it was for first-century Middle Eastern Jews like Joseph, Mary, Peter, and Paul.

Jesus also offers a radically different understanding of what it means to be a *leader*. His vision for leadership often parts ways with the typical American view of such things. For example:

In America, credentials qualify a person to lead. In Jesus, the chief qualification is character.

In America, what matters most are the results we produce. In Jesus, what matters most is the kind of people we are becoming.

In America, success is measured by material accumulation, power, and the positions that we hold. In Jesus, success is measured by material generosity, humility, and the people whom we serve.

In America, it is shameful to come in last and laudable to come in first. In Jesus, the first will be last and the last will be first.

In America, leaders make a name for themselves to become famous and sometimes treat Jesus as a means to that end. In Jesus, leaders make *his* name famous and treat their own positions, abilities, and influence as a means to *that* end.

In America, leaders crave recognition and credit. In Jesus, leaders think less of themselves and give credit to others.

In America, leaders compare and compete so they will flourish. In Jesus, leaders sacrifice and serve so others will flourish.

In America, leadership often means "*My* glory and happiness at *your* expense." In Jesus, leadership always means "*Your* growth and wholeness at *my* expense."

In America, the strong and powerful rise to the top. In Jesus, the meek inherit the earth.

The apostle Paul enjoyed great professional success and all the position, power, and recognition that a first-century rabbi could have dreamed of, yet he declared:

> But whatever gain I had, I counted as loss for the sake of Christ. Indeed, I count everything as loss because of the surpassing worth of knowing Christ Jesus my Lord. (Philippians 3:7–8)

And also:

> For the foolishness of God is wiser than men, and the weakness of God is stronger than men.
>
> For consider your calling … not many of you were wise according to worldly standards, not many were powerful, not many were of noble birth. But God chose what is foolish in the world to shame the wise; God chose what is weak in the world to shame the strong; God chose what

is low and despised in the world, even things that
are not, to bring to nothing things that are, so
that no human being might boast in the presence
of God. (1 Corinthians 1:25–29)

The record of Scripture confirms Paul's words to be true. Time
after time, the greatest and most influential leaders were imperfect,
uncredentialed men and women who would never be candidates
for our "Who's Who" and VIP lists.

Joseph, who was disowned by his brothers and thrown into an
Egyptian prison, later became the prime minister of Egypt. Noah,
a man who got drunk and passed out naked, rescued all the species
on earth from extinction. Abraham, at times a cowardly husband
and dysfunctional father, became the spiritual forerunner of all
who have faith. Isaiah, a preacher who was rejected by his contemporaries and sawed in half at his execution, became one of the most
influential voices in the history of the world. David, the youngest
of seven brothers and son of an obscure shepherd, became the king
of Israel and writer of over half the Psalms.

Peter, a hotheaded fisherman and erratic disciple who denied
Jesus three times, later became a bold truth teller who courageously
gave up everything for Jesus and was crucified upside down. Mary,
the unwed teenage girl from a small town, became the mother
of God's Son. Ruth the foreigner, Rahab the prostitute, and
Bathsheba the adulteress were honorably included in the family
tree of Jesus. Paul, once a blasphemer and persecutor and bully and

racist toward Gentiles, became apostle to the Gentiles and writer of one-third of the New Testament.

And then there was Jesus, who came to his own—but whose own did not receive him—who had nothing in his appearance that we should desire him, who died on a trash heap as a condemned criminal. Through this excruciating loss, Jesus *won* salvation for billions of souls and prepared the way for all things to be made new. Now and forevermore, the government of the whole universe rests squarely on the shoulders of the One who was despised and rejected by men.

Indeed, the most impactful, life-giving, and lasting leadership rests firmly on the shoulders of weakness. *God chose the weak things …*

… including me. How often I have pleaded, as the apostle Paul did, for the Lord to remove my thorns, my struggles, and the obstacles that beset me! Yet it has been in these very weaknesses and challenges, even heartbreaks, that God has revealed his power, strength, and sufficiency. Although the thorns are painful, they are a gift of grace to grow me into the kind of leader that I could never become without them.

In the pages that follow, we will look at eight common thorns through a biblical lens: unfulfilled ambition, isolation, criticism, envy, insecurity, anticlimax, opposition, and suffering. Depending on how we respond to them, these challenges will either make us or break us as leaders.

Whether your leadership takes the form of pastoring, parenting, mentoring, shepherding, writing, steering an organization, or championing a movement, I pray that the insights from this book will help you live and lead from weakness to strength.

Grace and peace,
Scott Sauls
Nashville, Tennessee

"And do you seek great things for yourself? Seek them not."

Jeremiah 45:5

Chapter 1

Ambition: The Catastrophe of Success

Sometimes the most loving thing God can do is to give you your dream job and then take it away from you.

The phone call came in 2007. At the time, I was in my fourth year pastoring and leading a growing, energetic, missional church in Saint Louis, Missouri. As a leader, I felt fulfilled. I met regularly with a couple of local pastors—Darrin and Andrew—who were becoming like brothers, and we were dreaming about how we could bless our city together. I got to teach preaching classes to students at Covenant Seminary, and that was a joy. Our daughters loved their schools and their friends and were enjoying their childhood. Our friendships were deep and meaningful. Grandma and

Grandpa lived just two miles away, and we were just a half day's drive from the rest of our extended family. Our intentions were to stay in this place doing this work together with these people for the rest of our days.

And then New York City called.

I had been a church planter and pastor for just over a decade. It is fair to say that Tim Keller, the founding pastor of New York's Redeemer Presbyterian Church, had influenced my preaching, pastoring, and ministerial vision more than everybody else combined. Ever since seminary, I had carefully studied Tim's teaching, vision, and leadership. Along with this self-directed "distance learning" from a "faculty" of one came a growing attraction to ministry amid the urban core.

Tim had heard about me through Redeemer's executive director, Bruce Terrell. The two of them were searching for a senior leader for the church's vast network of small groups. With the role also came the possibility of entering Redeemer's preaching rotation and, if the leading and preaching went well, becoming one of Tim's eventual successors (the succession for the five-thousand-person Manhattan church would roll out into four neighborhood-based, reproducing, and connected congregations, each with its own lead pastor).

After nearly six months of prayer and counseling and wrestling through the implications of moving our family to New York City, Patti and I accepted the call. In almost no time, we sold just about everything and moved our family of four into an 850-square-foot, two-bedroom, one-bath apartment on Manhattan's Upper West

Side. We ended up falling in love with New York, Redeemer, and the community God had placed around us. The small groups ministry reached a record participation level, and I was invited into the preaching rotation. After four years of being shaped and groomed for long-term ministry in the city, I was selected to be one of the four lead pastors.

The first time I heard John Wesley's famous "Covenant Prayer" was at the lead pastor commissioning service. The prayer is as follows:

> I am no longer my own, but yours. Put me to what you will, rank me with whom you will; put me to doing, *put me to suffering*; let me be employed for you, or *laid aside* for you, exalted for you, or *brought low* for you; let me be full, *let me be empty*, let me have all things, *let me have nothing*: I freely and wholeheartedly yield all things to your pleasure and disposal. And now, glorious and blessed God, Father, Son, and Holy Spirit, you are mine and I am yours. So be it. And the covenant now made on earth, let it be ratified in heaven. Amen. (emphasis added)

Pay attention to the sections that aren't usually voiced in public prayer. Who would pray to be brought low? Who asks for suffering? As Wesley's words were prayed that night over the four of us, I did not realize how prophetic the "surrender" parts would be for Patti, our daughters, and me. Within just one year, Redeemer's future plans would change. For reasons related to timing, resources, sustainability, and strategy, it became clear to the elders that Redeemer would need to reduce its plan at the time from four congregations to three, and, therefore, from four lead pastor/future successors to three. Nobody had planned for it to work out this way, but sadly, it did. Although Tim and the elders explored several options to ensure that all four of the original lead pastors remained part of Redeemer's future, after much prayer and counsel, one of us ended up resigning. That person was me. Given the circumstances, the decision felt like the right thing to do, but it still felt like the death of a dream.

In retrospect, I can see many reasons why God gave me my "dream job" in my "dream city" for a time—only to take it all away. One reason is that my current role at Christ Presbyterian Church in Nashville has, in just five years, far exceeded any previous dreaming I had done about other roles in other cities. We are now, more than we could have ever imagined, *home* in Nashville. And in a way, we have been "given back" the dream job … but also much more.

Christ Presbyterian, it turns out, was instrumental in sending Tim and Kathy to New York City to *start* Redeemer almost three decades ago. And now, having been influenced by Tim's leadership and vision more than ever after serving alongside him for five years, I am able to bring many of the valuable things I learned in New York to Nashville, which, for all intents and purposes, is *becoming* the type of city we left.

Even the *New York Times* has referred to Nashville as "The Third Coast" because of its creative, entrepreneurial, culture-making, and urbanizing trajectory. Formerly known as the Buckle of the Bible Belt, Nashville is swiftly becoming the Athens of the South—a bustling and energetic city whose influence reaches far beyond its own borders. I now understand more fully what Tim said to me in our final breakfast before we left New York: "Scott, we are sad to see you go. But it makes a lot of sense. You are going *to* Nashville *from* Nashville's future."

Reflecting on Wesley's prayer, I realized the New York experience also brought home the truth that I am not my own but have been bought with a price … and that God's ambition for my life, whether I understand it or not, is always superior to any ambitions that I might have for my life. Indeed, it is God's prerogative to do with my life, my family, and my ministry whatever God chooses.

"Put me to what you will … let me be employed for you, or laid aside for you." Thank you, John Wesley. And thank you to the suffering Job and the suffering Jesus. "The LORD gave and the LORD has taken away; blessed be the name of the LORD" (Job 1:21). "Father … not my will, but yours, be done" (Luke 22:42).

The New York experience also taught me a lot about the nature of ambition, which can be godly and pure but can also be self-serving and corrupt. It taught me that I am, on the one hand, a bit like Peter, who, wanting to please his Lord, gladly left everything to follow him (Matthew 19:27–29). I am similarly a bit like Paul, who made it his ambition to please Jesus, whether away or at home (2 Corinthians 5:9).

On the other hand, I am also a bit like Simon the sorcerer. Do you remember him? Simon was a man whose ambitions, unlike the ambitions of Peter and Paul, were self-serving and corrupt. Simon wasn't interested in Jesus using *him* as a servant for God's glory. Instead, Simon wanted to use *Jesus* as a servant for *Simon's* glory:

> When Simon saw that the Spirit was given through the laying on of the apostles' hands, he offered them money, saying, "Give me this power also, so that anyone on whom I lay my hands may receive the Holy Spirit." But Peter said to him, "May your silver perish with you, because you thought you could obtain the gift of God with money! You have neither part nor lot in this matter, for your heart is not right before God."
> (Acts 8:18–21)

I wish that it were difficult for me to relate to Simon. But, unfortunately, it is not. In some ways, my emotional attachment to New York revealed a similar heart in me, a heart that in certain ways was *not* right before God.

Leading up to my resignation, I had an emotional meltdown that lasted for over three months. I wasn't merely disappointed, which would have been legitimate; rather, I was devastated. I wasn't merely upset, which would also have been legitimate; rather, I was crushed. I couldn't sleep at night. I lost my appetite and, with it, somewhere between twenty and thirty pounds. I was anxious and depressed. Had I truly been openhanded toward God with *all* of my dreams and hopes and ambitions? Had I truly believed that the writing of my story belonged to God and not to me? If I had, then thoughts of walking away from my dream job, though deeply disappointing, would not have wrecked me to the degree that they did.

Looking back, I now believe that this experience was best not only for Redeemer and Christ Presbyterian but also for Patti, our girls, and me. This has to be true, if for no other reason than that it is impossible for God to shortchange any of his children. If we had access to everything that God knows and sees about us, then his ways would make perfect sense to us. For me in particular, it was an important wake-up call about two lessons that every leader must learn and relearn on a regular basis. Let me put them before you so you can think them through.

Lesson #1—Our Failures and Disappointments Reveal the State of Our Souls

My circumstance-triggered meltdown was at least in part because of idols of success, fame, and making a name for myself that had long been residing in my heart. Like hot water brings the tea out of a dry tea bag, the New York event became the context that exposed an ugly ambition in me. Somehow, I had come to believe that leading in a global city and pastoring thousands of people with Ivy League degrees and "important" jobs and household names were the things that would give me significance, justify my existence, and make me esteemed in the eyes of men. Subconsciously, I related to an anecdote that Donald Miller once told about the comedian Tom Arnold:

> I caught an interview with Tom Arnold regarding his book *How I Lost Five Pounds in Six Years*. The interviewer asked why he had written the book, and I was somewhat amazed at the honesty of Arnold's answer. The comedian stated that most entertainers are in show business because they are broken people, looking for affirmation. "The reason I wrote this book," Tom Arnold said, "is because I wanted something out there so people would tell me they liked me. It's the reason behind almost everything I do."[1]

Replace "comedian" with "pastor" and "show business" with "ministry," and you get exactly the same person with the same exact issues—only in a different setting and career path. Genuinely good endeavors like comedy and ministry (or the arts, or business, or entrepreneurism, or parenting, or healthcare, or education, or government, or what have you) become *broken* endeavors when we start depending on them to satisfy our thirst for love, esteem, applause, and approval in ways that only Jesus can.

We are famous in God's eyes through Jesus … and that should be enough.

Now that we're a few years beyond the New York experience, I hope that my heart and my ambitions are in a healthier place. I hope that my subconscious desire to be the hero of my own story—or *any kind* of hero, for that matter—is fading. I hope that my inmost desires are becoming more and more that Jesus would increase and I would decrease—and that I would be deeply satisfied in my role as a supporting actor in *his* story instead of wanting him to be a supporting actor in mine—oh, the horror! I hope that the next time my dreams and ambitions are disrupted or brought to a halt, for they surely will be at some point, I will be more prepared to surrender everything to God with an open hand as Job and Jesus did and to trust deeply the words of a wise old hymn:

> Whate'er my God ordains is right:
> Here shall my stand be taken;
> Though sorrow, need, or death be mine,
> Yet I am not forsaken.
> My Father's care is round me there;
> He holds me that I shall not fall:
> And so to him I leave it all.

All of that might seem highly abstract, but this kind of trust can find a concrete home in the heart of the believer. For instance, it might look like a friend of mine I will call Ted, an attorney who got pushed out of his firm not in spite of but *because of* his good and honest heart.

One day, Ted's supervisor called a private meeting with him. During that meeting, the supervisor told him that if he wanted to keep his job, he would have to fudge the truth about a particular client's assets. "If the truth about the client's assets became known by shareholders," the supervisor reasoned, "it would be the end of the client's business and, by extension, the end of a significant income stream coming into the law firm from that client."

Ted, from a place of loyalty to Jesus and a nonnegotiable commitment to keeping his integrity, respectfully refused to follow his supervisor's instructions. He was swiftly terminated from his job at the firm.

That's harsh enough. But there was more. It later became clear that Ted's supervisor, by secretly slandering him to potential future employers, got him blackballed by virtually every law firm in the city that was home to him and his family. This resulted in a long two years of unemployment, which had a deep, painful impact not only on Ted but also on his loving wife and three children.

Somewhere in the middle of those two years, I caught Ted before a church service. Jokingly, I asked him if he wanted me to go out and get a jug of gasoline and some matches so he and I could go set his former place of employment on fire, starting with his former supervisor's office.

Ted, with a witty smirk but also with a profoundly serious demeanor, looked me straight in the eye and uttered two words I will never forget:

"No retribution."

Like I said, what's on the inside—whatever has *always* been there—will come out under pressure.

How about us? When our dreams and ambitions die, when we lose influence or reputation or a dream job, or when we experience injustice and betrayal like my friend Ted did, what will be revealed about our hearts? Will our hearts show themselves to be "right before God"? As Jesus said, "Will there be faith on earth?" (see Luke 18:8).

Lesson #2—Our Successes and Achievements Are Poor Jesus Substitutes

If you find your happiness in yourself and your own achievements, you're bound to be disappointed. Consider how often you've let yourself down, for one thing. For another—well, C. S. Lewis was onto something when he said:

> Aim at heaven and you will get earth thrown in;
> aim at earth and you will get neither.[2]

I learned this the hard way when, for a season, I allowed ministry in a "notable" city among "notable" people to become an idol. I now see how foolish this thinking was. I see how right Francis Schaeffer was when he said that there are *no* little places and *no* little people. If Jesus would choose the small, obscure town of Bethlehem as his birthplace and the better-known (but only because of its bad reputation) town of Nazareth—"Can anything good come out of Nazareth?" (John 1:46)—as his temporal home, and if he could choose to build his kingdom chiefly through people who were *not* wise or powerful or of noble birth (1 Corinthians 1:26), how dare I act or think or believe otherwise as I minister in his name!

More recently, I have begun to learn Lewis's and Schaeffer's wisdom in more enjoyable, life-giving ways. Though Nashville and Christ Presbyterian have more similarities to than differences from New York and Redeemer, and though many would look at our current situation and call it a "success story," my perspective on success is quite different from what it has been in the past.

The past three years have been especially rich for us. Recently, Patti and I celebrated our twenty-third wedding anniversary. She can speak for herself, but I will tell you that my love for her is deeper now than it has ever been, and the thought of growing old with her is a happy thought. As those who know her best would say, she is the aroma of Christ and a carrier of the Spirit's fruit— others-oriented, approachable, thoughtful, lovely, and kind. Patti is not perfect, but she is beautifully solid. As they say, I married up.

Then there is our oldest daughter, Abby, who just completed her first year of college. Though still a teenager, there are some things that make her more "adult-like" than many full-fledged adults. When the crowd acts foolishly or hurtfully, she follows her convictions instead of the crowd. She spends volunteer time befriending children with special needs. Last summer, she served as a counselor at a camp for struggling and at-risk preteens. This summer, she gave her time and her heart to refugees.

Ellie, our younger daughter, just completed her first year of high school. Ellie is a hardworking, kindhearted girl who lights up a room with her kindness. She is aware of the people around her and helps others feel seen, cared for, and at home. She is not part of an exclusive clique, but, like her mother, she seeks to be a friend to all. She is compassionate, sensitive, and honest. We are very proud of the young lady she is becoming.

As for me, I am thriving professionally, perhaps now more than ever. Ever since we arrived, Christ Presbyterian Church has been blossoming around us. Our staff is unified, and morale is stronger than ever. Our elder meetings are forward-thinking, fun, lighthearted, and relational, even as we tend to serious matters of church business. We major in the majors and minor in the minors—in other words, we don't sweat the small stuff, and we take the serious stuff seriously. As the world measures success, we're successful. In five years, we have grown from having one Sunday service to three, and we've gone from one location to two. Seventy percent of our current members joined us within the last five years, and our newcomer gatherings are always full.

That's all great, and I once would have put all my rejoicing into those numbers. But that's not nearly as significant as how Christ Presbyterian serves its city. Like Redeemer in New York City, our church invests not chiefly in itself but in its city and the world. We focus not on our own preservation but on helping Christians engage thoughtfully with their neighbors and the culture about things that matter, integrate their faith with their work, and contribute meaningfully to the elevation of those who are poor, overlooked, underserved, and living in the margins.

Amidst all of it, I get to pastor and live among and be friends with some of the loveliest and most generous, life-giving, and remarkable people I have ever met.

At least for now, my life seems to be an embarrassment of riches.

As I think about all of these blessings, I am struck by Jesus's admonishment to his disciples precisely when their perceived "success" and "influence" *were at their peak*:

> The seventy-two returned with joy, saying, "Lord, even the demons are subject to us in your name!" And he said to them … "Behold, I have given you authority to tread on serpents and scorpions, and over all the power of the enemy, and nothing shall hurt you. Nevertheless, do not rejoice in this, that the spirits are subject to you, but rejoice that your names are written in heaven." (Luke 10:17–20)

Did you catch that?

When Jesus's disciples came to him with news of their extraordinary strength and influence and success, his response was to say, "Do *not* rejoice in that."

When God gives us success for a time, when he chooses to put the wind at our backs—by all means, we should enjoy the experience. But we mustn't hang our hats on it … because earthly success, in all its forms, comes to us as a gift from God and is also fleeting. Our Lord is telling us not to allow appetizers to replace the feast, or a single apple to replace the orchard, or a road sign to replace the destination to which it points. On this, Lewis again provides essential wisdom:

> It would seem that Our Lord finds our desires (that is, our ambitions) not too strong, but too weak. We are half-hearted creatures, fooling about with drink and sex and ambition when infinite joy is offered us, like an ignorant child wants to go on making mud pies in a slum because he cannot imagine what is meant by the offer of a holiday at the sea. We are far too easily pleased.[3]

We genuinely do find ourselves satisfied with what amounts to small, insignificant, self-pleasing trifles. Lewis's perspective reminds us that no self-serving ambition has the ability to satisfy the vastness of the human soul made in the image of God. As Augustine aptly said, the Lord has made us for himself. Our hearts will be restless until they find their rest in him.

This perspective from Lewis is also our safeguard from what the famous playwright Tennessee Williams called "The Catastrophe of Success." Williams understood that things like momentum, influence, and position, and being known and being celebrated, are fine in themselves, but he also knew that none of these things can sustain us in the long run. Reflecting on his instant success after the release of *The Glass Menagerie*, his blockbuster Broadway play, Williams wrote:

> I was snatched out of virtual oblivion and thrust into sudden prominence … I sat down and looked about me and was suddenly very depressed … I lived on room service. But in this, too, there was a disenchantment … I soon found myself becoming indifferent to people. A well of cynicism rose in me … I got so sick of hearing people say, "I loved your play!" that I could not say thank you any more … I no longer felt any pride in the play itself but began to dislike it, probably because I felt too lifeless inside ever to create another. I was walking around dead in my shoes … You know, then, that the public Somebody you are when you "have a name" is a fiction created with mirrors.[4]

Tennessee Williams's story, as well as the story of every person who has experienced the anticlimax of having gotten to the end of the rainbow and finding no pot of gold is there after all, confirms a universal truth for every human heart: Only Jesus, whose rule and whose peace shall never cease to increase (Isaiah 9:7), can sustain us. Only Jesus, whose resurrection assures us that he is—and forever will be—making all things new, can fulfill our deepest desires and give us a happily-ever-after conclusion. Only Jesus can make everything sad come untrue.[5] Only Jesus can ensure a future in which every chapter will be better than the one before.[6] Only Jesus can give us the glory and the soaring strength of an eagle (Isaiah 40:31). Only Jesus, whose name is above every name and at whose name every knee will bow, can give us a name that will endure forever (Philippians 2:9–10; Isaiah 56:5).

All that should help us realize that making much of *his* name is a far superior ambition than making a name for ourselves. Apart from Jesus, all men and women—even the most ambitious and successful and strong—will wither away like a vapor. "People are grass. The grass withers, the flower fades, but the word of our God will stand forever" (Isaiah 40:7–8).

Lastly, if this isn't enough to give us a healthier, humbler perspective on our ambitions, perhaps this observation from Anne Lamott will:

> One hundred years from now?
> All new people.[7]

"In the spring of the year, the time when kings go out to battle.... David arose from his couch ... he saw from the roof a woman bathing.... So David sent messengers and took her, and she came to him, and he lay with her."

2 Samuel 11:1–2, 4

Chapter 2

Isolation: The Soil for Collapse

The Bible knows the human condition well. It reveals that in each of us there is potential for great good *and* potential for tremendous evil.

I look back on my days in graduate school with a bit of awe as I see how God has used many of my classmates for good. Two of them are pastors with me at our church in Nashville. Another worships at our church and has spent over a decade making an impact on college students at the university where he serves and across the nation as well. Other former classmates have become authors, teachers, counselors, pastors, and thought leaders.

Sadly, there are also a few from our class whose stories have included adultery, divorce, abandoning their families, using illegal drugs, and leaving Christianity altogether.

It grieves me to see the moral collapse of those alongside whom I had once studied, prayed, worshipped, served, loved, and dreamed about the future of Christianity. This reminds me of a story I heard about a famous pastor that was told by his former intern. One time at a staff meeting, the intern recalls the famous pastor informing the entire staff that Satan has the power to tempt him in any number of ways but that there is one area of his life that Satan will never touch: his marriage.

According to the intern, the pastor was caught in bed with a mistress less than one year after that staff meeting.

For pastors, and all leaders, stories like these should cause us to pause and humbly admit our weaknesses and temptations. It is not only ancient biblical accounts that tell us how frail we are. It is also the stories of moral collapse "from the top" that happen every single day—even among the most well-intended Christian leaders. There is potential in every leader, *even the most virtuous ones*, to become caught in unimaginable transgression.

Think about it. If Abraham, the father of all who have faith, could offer up his wife *twice* to be sexually used by unsavory men in order to save his own hide, aren't we also capable of preserving ourselves while making others vulnerable? If Jacob, the father of the twelve tribes of Israel, could for many years live out a lie concerning his birthright, aren't we also capable of becoming liars? If Rahab, who is listed as an ancestor of Jesus, gave up her body as a prostitute, aren't we also capable of immoral thoughts and behaviors?

If Peter, one of the twelve apostles and writer of two New Testament letters, could fall into xenophobic behavior *after* Jesus had restored him to ministry because he was afraid of what the other xenophobes might say, and if Barnabas, widely known as "the son of encouragement," could stumble right alongside him, aren't we also capable of excluding those whom Jesus embraces? If King David, who gave us beautiful worship poetry in the Psalms and who was identified by the Lord himself as "a man after God's own heart," could abuse his power by taking Bathsheba—also the daughter of one of his most loyal friends—to sleep with him and then scheming to have her husband, also a loyal friend, killed to cover it up, aren't we also capable of abusing our power to get from others whatever we want?

To these, we could also add many of the titans from church history. John Calvin participated in the execution of a man whose crime was disagreement with Christian doctrine. Martin Luther made statements that were racist and anti-Semitic. Jonathan Edwards owned slaves until the day he died. Martin Luther King Jr. was unfaithful to his wife as he traveled the country preaching from the Bible and leading the civil rights movement.

On the one hand, I find the stories of such leaders strangely encouraging. If there is hope for these, then there is also hope for someone like me. On the other hand, their stories, their foolishness, and their sin should instruct us and help us live differently.

Their stories teach us the importance of guarding our hearts, because our hearts, especially when we think they are not vulnerable or susceptible to sin, are more vulnerable and susceptible than ever.

"Let anyone who thinks that he stands take heed," said the apostle, "lest he fall. No temptation has overtaken you that is not *common* to man" (1 Corinthians 10:12–13).

Are you a leader who thinks you are not vulnerable? Are you like the person who looks at the acorn and thinks that such a little thing could never become an oak tree, or a forest, or a forest fire? The sin in our hearts is the acorn. It has the power, if not crushed, to germinate, to become a sprout ... and then a tree ... and then an entire forest.

This is in part why Jesus, in the Sermon on the Mount, warned not only against adultery but against lust in the heart. This is also why he warned not only against murder but against a grudge in the heart. Every adulterous fling begins with a "harmless" thought or glance, and every murderous rampage begins with a seemingly insignificant grudge.

Wherever our hearts are vulnerable, it is essential to crush the acorn before it becomes a sprout, to dig up the sprout before it grows into a tree, to chop down the tree before it becomes a forest, to plow the forest before it takes over more and more land.

God said to Cain, "Sin is crouching at your door ... You must rule over it" (Genesis 4:7). Master the sin, Cain, lest the sin gain mastery over you. Crush the sin, Cain, lest the sin end up crushing you and those around you.

As the wise Puritan John Owen said, "Be killing sin, or sin will be killing you."[1]

And then there is Pink, the rock star, who sings words that should be a daily refrain for every leader—or human being, for that matter—who is self-aware:

I'm a hazard to myself.
Don't let me get me.[2]

This was King David's problem. His adultery and murder began with what we might call "smaller" or "lesser" sins. First, he grew complacent in his duty as a leader. We are told that the Bathsheba incident occurred during the time when kings go out to war. Israel's armies, which included Bathsheba's husband, Uriah, were away fighting the Ammonites. But David, who could have been fighting with his men and leading the charge, sat at home isolated in his castle in the same way that many compromised leaders isolate themselves from community and accountability. It is also significant that Scripture says David, when he saw and sent for Bathsheba, had been napping on his couch in the middle of the day. As the men of Israel were out risking their lives at war, sweating and bleeding and putting their lives on the line and exhausted from battle, David, their king, was by himself in the comfort of his castle taking an afternoon nap.

Why did David exempt himself from fighting alongside his men? One can only speculate. But perhaps he did so for the same reason he would send for, and then take for himself, somebody else's wife: David thought he had earned the right to do whatever he pleased. After all, he had spent several years running as a refugee and living in caves to escape the jealous, murderous Saul; he had rescued Israel in the slaying of Goliath; he had endured the capture of his own family members at war; and he had lamented the death in battle of his best friend Jonathan. Furthermore, he had endured wrongful shame and ridicule from his wife Michal; he had been a man of faithfulness and integrity and prayer; he had given refuge and shelter to Jonathan's orphaned son with special needs, Mephibosheth; and he had fought more battles than just about anybody. Through all of these things, hadn't he earned the *right* to enjoy some leisure and to live however he wanted to live?

"After all that I have done for these people and for this nation," David might have said to himself, "what's the harm in a little bit of illicit sex on the side? What's the harm in a little bit of cover-up when she reveals that she is expecting my child? What's the harm in arranging for the death of Uriah to cover our tracks and create plausible deniability so the world will think that the child belongs to Uriah instead of me? I have the stability of an entire nation on my shoulders. Things would erupt into turmoil if this got out. I'm plagued by stress. I feel so much pressure. I feel so alone. Nobody knows what it's like to be me. *I deserve this.*"

It's what Tim Keller once called "magisterial self-pity." Forgetting the privilege of leadership, we come to view ourselves as victims instead of servants, as being above the law instead of living under it like everybody else, as being entitled instead of being grateful recipients of an undeserved grace.

And so I will ask again, have you ever thought that Satan couldn't get to you too? Have you ever said with Peter—the disciple who would later deny and betray Jesus not once, but three times—"Even though they all fall away, I will not" (Mark 14:29)? Have you ever thought that you aren't capable of denial and betrayal and adultery and murder and other such things?

You are. And I am too.

That part of us that thinks it's harmless to flirt with lust, gossip, greed, or anger—just so long as we don't get into bed with it—is the fool in us. Quite possibly, we could end up in bed with it sooner than we think.

In the past two years, five of my pastor friends have lost their ministries. Not just one or two friends, though that would be tragic enough. Five of them have fallen.

Five.

Most of these pastors are widely known beyond their local contexts as authors, conference speakers, and movement leaders. From the outside, they appeared to be at their peak.

For reasons beyond my ability to understand, God has graciously protected me from moral collapse over the years—so far. Knowing the fragility and fickleness of my own heart, sometimes I am perplexed at how this could be. Why them and not me? Sometimes I wonder if, under different circumstances, I, too, would collapse morally. As the famous hymn goes, "Prone to wander, Lord, I feel it ..." Indeed, *I feel* my proneness to wander every single day. The lustful, murderous David and the cowardly, self-protecting Peter always lurk within me.

There is another person from Scripture who lurks in me. He is not the adulterer or the murderer. Neither is he the coward or the self-protector. He is the one whose name means "my God is the Lord." He lives and serves and leads courageously, goes against the grain, and would rather die while being faithful to God than be rich, comfortable, and unfaithful. He is the prophet who publicly takes on hundreds of false prophets and wins. He is the man of faith who prays rain down from the sky and brings hope to a hopeless widow. He is the man of God who speaks truth to power only to have a bounty put on his head by Jezebel, the paragon of evil herself, who will stop at nothing to have him discredited, silenced, and destroyed.

This prophet's name is Elijah. He, too, succumbs to the pressure and isolation of leadership—and not by falling into sin, but by falling into despair. Though he has seen much victory and experienced abundant provision from the Lord, Elijah grows tired and weary. When he hears the news that Jezebel wants him killed, he enters a dark season of floundering faith and deep depression (1 Kings 19:1–18). He collapses into himself, hides in a cave, and comes to believe that he is the *only* servant of Yahweh who remains. Then, at his lowest point, Elijah prays the prayer that, no doubt, many other leaders have prayed:

> [Elijah] went a day's journey into the wilderness and came and sat down under a broom tree. And he asked that he might die, saying, "It is enough; now, O LORD, take away my life, for I am no better than my fathers." (1 Kings 19:4)

Charles Haddon Spurgeon, the great Baptist "Prince of Preachers," once told his students that if they could be happy doing something besides ministry, they should do it. I'm sure there were several reasons why Spurgeon gave this advice. But the reason his advice makes sense to me is this ...

> *Being a pastor—or any kind of leader—can be very, very hard.*

In my midtwenties, while studying to become a pastor, I came across a suicide note published in the local newspaper. It had been written by a local pastor, and it included these haunting words:

> God forgive me for not being any stronger than I am. But when a minister becomes clinically depressed, there are very few places where he can turn to for help ... It feels as if I'm sinking farther and farther into a downward spiral of depression. I feel like a drowning man, trying frantically to lift up my head to take just one more breath. But one way or another, I know I am going down.[3]

The writer was a promising young pastor of a large church in Saint Louis, Missouri. Having secretly battled depression for a long time and having sought help through Scripture reading, prayer, therapy, and medication, his will to claw through yet another day was gone. In his darkest hour, the young leader decided he would rather join the angels than continue facing demons for years to come.

Some of those "demons," it turned out, were high-powered members of his church whose expectations of him were impossibly high.

Not many months after this man's tragic suicide, another Saint Louis pastor asphyxiated himself because of a similar secret depression.

As an aspiring pastor myself, the news of these two pastors' suicides rocked my world. How could these men—both gifted leaders who believed in Jesus, preached grace, and comforted others with gospel hope—end up *losing hope* for themselves?

As more people heard the stories of these two men, it became clear that both of them shared an all-too-common reality for pastors. Both had allowed themselves to become relationally isolated ... *especially* in their churches.

They had plenty of *adoring fans*.

But they had few, if any, *actual friends*.

In his suicide note, the first pastor said that he felt trapped. He was isolated and depressed, but he didn't tell anyone because he thought it would ruin his ministry. He had come to believe that pastors and leaders weren't allowed to be weak. Nor were they allowed to be human, like everybody else.

Unfortunately, the two pastors from Saint Louis are not rare. Many of us pastors have fallen into the emotional abyss—not in spite of the fact that we are in ministry but *because* we are in ministry, just as many leaders also fall into the emotional abyss not in spite of their leadership positions but because of them.

Studies show that pastors experience anxiety and depression at a rate that is disproportionately high compared to the rest of the population. Because of the unique pressures associated with spiritual warfare, unrealistic expectations from congregants and oneself, the freedom many feel to criticize and gossip about pastors with zero accountability (especially in the digital age), failure to take time off for rest and replenishment, marriage and family tensions as a result of the demands of ministry, financial strain, and self-comparison, pastors are prime candidates for relational isolation, emotional turmoil, and moral collapse.

Studies also show that some pastors face unreasonable, even impossible, demands placed on them by their people. I am *not* one of those pastors, thanks to a church that receives my gifts and acknowledges my limitations. All in all, the people of Christ Presbyterian Church in Nashville, Tennessee, treat me with extraordinary love and understanding. But, sadly, not all pastors are as lucky as I am.

Dr. Thom Rainer, a leading pastoral ministry expert, conducted a survey asking church members what they expected from their pastors. Specifically, Dr. Rainer wanted to know the *minimum* amount of time church members believed their pastors should give each week to various areas of ministry, including prayer, sermon preparation, outreach and evangelism, counseling, administrative tasks, visiting the sick, community involvement, denominational engagement, church meetings, worship services, and so on. On average, the *minimum* amount of time church members expected their pastors to give to the ministry was 114 hours per week.[4] That equates to working sixteen-hour days, seven days a week!

As in all positions of leadership, ministry can take a toll on the pastor's family. When church members don't like the pastor's sermon, when they don't like the direction of the church, when they think the music is too loud (or too soft), when they believe the pastor should wear a suit instead of jeans (or jeans instead of a suit), when the pastor messes with someone's "sacred cow," the pastor's spouse can become a sounding board for disgruntled church members.

Second only to those who are married to public officials, no spouse in the world is thrust into the line of "friendly fire" more than the pastor's spouse. For this very reason, it took my wife, Patti, forty-five minutes to say yes to my marriage proposal! The pastor's spouse can also experience loneliness: in some churches, the pastor is expected to be as available to the church as he is to his own family.

Then there are the pastor's kids—the "PKs"—those little ones who are sometimes expected to behave like mature grown-ups. Consciously and subconsciously, the pastor's kids don't believe that they are allowed to be *kids* like their peers. They feel a unique pressure to please, to play the part, to be on their best behavior at all times. For some, this pressure leads to perfectionism and stress. For others, it leads to rebellion. It can be difficult for PKs to blend into the crowd and develop their own identities and personalities because, unlike most kids, they live their lives in the public eye.

Sharing a last name with the pastor fuels a lot of unspoken (and sometimes spoken) pressure for a young person to navigate.

So why am I telling you all of this? For a few reasons ...

First, if you are a pastor or a family member of a pastor, I want you to know that the pressure and isolation you sometimes feel is normal. Yours is a unique calling from God—an unspeakable privilege, to be sure—but it is also sometimes unspeakably *hard*.

Satan is not fond of your life's mission. He is threatened by it, so he is going to attack you. Sometimes he will attack and accuse you through the very people God has given you to shepherd and love. When this happens, please don't get cynical about God's people. Stay hopeful about the church like Paul did with Corinth. Look at the cracked seed, and envision the flower or the fruit tree. Even when you are unfairly criticized, look for a nugget or two of truth in the criticism. You may find something fresh to repent of ... and every opportunity to repent is also an opportunity to draw near to Jesus anew.

But we pastors must also admit that there are times when *we*, and not congregants who struggle with our leadership, are the actual problem. When we feel under pressure, we can become sensitive, defensive, snippy, and even aggressive—unless we are careful to guard our hearts. As pastors, we are vulnerable to paint ourselves as victims on the one hand or to become bullies or crooks or adulterers on the other.

What should we do when criticism comes and the criticism is actually fair, when we have hurt people, compromised integrity, or even disqualified ourselves from leading? Our task is to apply the things we have taught others ... to take full ownership of what we have done, to repent to God, and to make restitution to those who have suffered because of our decisions wherever possible. To learn more about this, read on; the next chapter focuses on responding to criticism constructively—whether the criticism is constructive or not.

But this isn't all. Our task is also to do battle against the guilt and shame that haunt us, the guilt and shame that linger even after we have owned up to God and made restitution to and sought forgiveness from those who have suffered because of our actions. Even if the consequence of our actions ends up being the loss of our ministry, Jesus can still work within us. I dare say that he is eager to do so.

If there was hope for Paul in his coveting (Romans 7), hope for Peter in his racial insensitivity and cowardice and denials of Jesus (Mark 14:66–72; Galatians 2), and hope for David after his adultery and murder (Psalm 51), then we can be sure that no matter how far we have fallen, we have not fallen beyond the reach of God's grace and concern. Jesus came for sinners, not for heroes. Perhaps the recognition that we are not heroes can be an occasion—maybe the first one in quite some time—to fall into his healing arms. Though his rod and staff of discipline may seem harsh for a time, may they become our source of comfort down the line ... just as they did for David (Psalm 23).

Pastors and all other leaders—let's pray for each other. Though the spirit is willing, our flesh is weak. Let's never get past our need for Jesus to carry us. Without him, we are vulnerable. We are vulnerable when our ministries and spheres of leadership are struggling, and—as the moral collapse of my five friends attests—we are vulnerable when our efforts seem to be soaring and accomplishing great things. Paul called this "living in plenty" and "living in want." Regardless of our situation, we can do all things *through Christ*, who gives us strength (Philippians 4:11–13). Let's believe this together. And let's hold each other's arms up when we struggle to believe.

If you are not a pastor, I beg you to remove your pastor from the pedestal where you and others may have been tempted to place him. Under the right circumstances, we pastors can be some of the best friends and advocates. But we pastors make very, very bad heroes. Turning us into heroes not only hurts our churches; it also hurts us.

It hurts a lot more to fall from a pedestal than it does from the ground where everybody else is standing. Plus, only Jesus belongs on a pedestal. We pastors are shepherds ... but we are also sheep just like everybody else. We have struggles and fears. We sometimes get depressed and anxious. We can be unsure of ourselves, and we go through seasons wondering if we really belong in ministry. Many of us are more frustrated with ourselves than you could ever be with us. Sometimes we see our hypocrisy a lot more clearly than you do. Sometimes we grow more tired of ourselves than you grow tired of us. And sometimes we get puffed up and need a faithful Nathan, just like David did, to help us see how we fail to live up to the things that we preach.

For these and other reasons, part of my daily prayer includes this:

> Father in heaven,
> Always grant me character
> that is greater than my gifts
> and humility
> that is greater than my influence.
> Amen.

If you are a congregant, please *don't stop* holding us pastors to a high standard. Don't let us off the hook from the high calling to lead with love, joy, peace, patience, kindness, goodness, faithfulness, gentleness, and self-control. But as you do, please remember that we need those things from you too. All of us are incomplete works in process who are on a journey toward perfection. But we haven't reached it yet. What Herman Melville said seems to fit:

> Heaven have mercy on us all—Presbyterians and
> Pagans alike—for we are all somehow dreadfully
> cracked about the head, and sadly need mending.[5]

The best grace you could give to pastors is this: Pray for us, live in community with us, and insist that we live in community with you. Please don't put us on pedestals or treat us as heroes. Rather, recognize us as fellow sojourners with you. When this happens, the chances of our becoming isolated and domineering and snippy and untruthful and full of ourselves and greedy and adulterous—and whatever else could eventually disqualify us—will be significantly reduced.

Thanks for allowing me to speak honestly here. I suspect that whatever kind of leader you are or want to be, some part of what is written in this chapter resonates with you. Perhaps you, too, have been sobered by stories of emotional and moral collapse. Perhaps you, too, are lamenting over friends who have fallen.

And perhaps you, too, wonder why it was them instead of you.

"There came out a man of the family of the house of Saul, whose name was Shimei … and as he came he cursed continually. And he threw stones at David … Abishai the son of Zeruiah said to the king, 'Why should this dead dog curse my lord the king? Let me go over and take off his head.' But the king said, '… If he is cursing because the LORD has said to him, "Curse David," who then shall say, "Why have you done so?"'"

2 Samuel 16:5–6, 9–10

Chapter 3

Criticism: An Invitation to Self-Reflection

I hate it when people criticize me.

Yet being criticized is to be expected when you are an influencer or a leader. Even the best parents routinely get criticized by their children, bosses by their employees, coaches by their players, athletes and artists by their fans, teachers by their students, and pastors by their congregants. If we are unable to handle criticism, we may want to consider doing something different with our lives.

Over the years, I have gotten better about receiving criticism from the people around me. When the criticism is fair, it actually helps me see my blind spots, address my weaknesses, and improve my efforts at loving and leading those around me. However, when the criticism is *not* fair, I can sometimes react in a negative and defensive way. And, honestly, I sometimes react that way when the criticism *is* fair.

Recently, a man who was traveling through Nashville and had visited our church sent me a public criticism on Twitter, telling me all the things that, in his "humble opinion," were wrong about my sermon. Feeling defensive and irritated, I foolishly retaliated with a criticism of my own, along with a Bible verse to justify my response. The man then sent *five* more messages on Twitter, piling on more criticism, taking my words out of context, and putting words in my mouth. I then responded a second time, again in a way that was not helpful.

My friend and unofficial big brother, Pastor Scotty Smith, saw the exchange between the church visitor and me and swiftly sent me a text message that said, "Scott, dear brother, you forgot that you're not supposed to wrestle with pigs."

Scotty's text was not intended as an insult to the man on Twitter. Rather, he was reminding me of a phrase that he and I had picked up from an article by leadership expert Carey Nieuwhof about healthy leadership. "Don't wrestle with pigs" is another way of saying that when people try to pick a fight with you or when they seem bent on criticizing you no matter what you say or do, it's usually best simply not to engage them. Why? Because when leaders "wrestle with pigs," we both get dirty—but it's only the pig who enjoys it. We also run the risk of ourselves becoming pig-headed in the process.

There is another disadvantage to "wrestling with pigs." When we fight back—instead of seeking to defuse the situation by not responding or by answering gently—we condition ourselves to reject *all* criticism, even the kind that *is* fair. We do this to our own peril.

As I said in the previous chapter, in each of us is the potential for great good and potential for exceptional evil. We are, at the same time, both Dr. Jekyll and Mr. Hyde. Scripture puts words to this dual reality in multiple ways. We are, at the same time, saints and transgressors, old man and new man, flesh and spirit. We are, as Luther said, *simul iustus et peccator*—at the same time righteous and sinner. This means that we are at all times capable of heroic love *and* unspeakable evil. Even the apostle Paul, one of the greatest Christian leaders who ever lived, recognized this about himself as he wrote in his letter to the Romans:

> I do not understand my own actions. For I do not do what I want, but I do the very thing I hate.... For I know that nothing good dwells in me, that is, in my flesh. For I have the desire to do what is right, but not the ability to carry it out. For I do not do the good I want, but the evil I do not want is what I keep on doing....
>
> When I want to do right, evil lies close at hand. For I delight in the law of God, in my inner being, but I see in my members another law waging war against the law of my mind and making me captive to the law of sin. (Romans 7:15, 18–19, 21–23)

Thankfully for all of us, this was not the end of the story for Paul. Having been brought low by his sin, he went on in the next chapter to provide the hope-filled solution to his (and our) problem with sin. In Christ, who has redeemed us from the curse of God's law, there is no condemnation. Christ, who is our legal advocate before the judgment seat of God, also gives his Spirit to dwell inside of us. The Spirit helps us to pray when we don't know how, directs our minds toward the things of the Spirit and away from the things of the flesh, and reminds us that nothing in all creation will *ever* be able to separate us from his love (Romans 8).

This reality that we find in the pages of Scripture—that God responds to our sin with reassurance instead of shame, kindness instead of punishment, mercy instead of judgment, and love instead of abandonment—presses us to consider why we would ever want to continue sinning. If it is true that it is not our repentance that leads God to be kind but God's kindness that leads us to repent (Romans 2:4), then why would we ever consider *not* repenting of our sin as a viable option? If God has, through the perfect life and sacrificial, atoning death of Jesus, moved our judgment day from the future to the past, why would we ever think it right or good or beneficial to continue living in ways that are worthy of judgment?

Sin is absurd and futile, especially for Christians who are aware of the love and redeeming grace of God through Jesus. It is absurd and futile because we know that sin is not only an act of rebellion against the *law* of God. Even worse, it is an act of hatred against the *love* of God.

This was why King David, reflecting on his adultery, murder, and abuse of power, wrote about how his sins had brought him no joy but instead caused his bones to feel crushed and his spirit sapped of joy (Psalm 51:8, 12). Giving in to his idols had afflicted him, tormented his soul, blocked his vision, enveloped him with grief, and wasted him physically (Psalm 31:6–10).

To sin against the law of God is to sin against the love of God. Whenever we sin against God, we also sin against ourselves. We cannot be happy and healthy and whole outside the blessed boundaries of God's law any more than a fish can be happy and healthy and whole outside of the water. For those created in God's image, his law is our road map for how to "image" him. His law is our design and our natural habitat.

Eugene Peterson tells it true in *The Message*: "Trivialize even the smallest item in God's Law and you will only have trivialized yourself" (Matthew 5:19–20).

Although the wisdom of adhering to our design may seem obvious, we still need help. We need the wisdom of Scripture to anchor us daily in the things that are right, good, and true. Our hearts are deceptive and frail, and they are therefore capable of justifying even the worst thoughts and words and actions. Our hearts are, like David's and Paul's, "prone to wander, Lord, I feel it, prone to leave the God I love." We need people in our lives to remind us that we have not arrived yet. Because we are not yet what we are meant to be, we all need honest voices in our lives to help us see in ourselves the sin that we cannot see and to confront us when we need confronting.

In her excellent book *Hope Has Its Reasons*, Rebecca Pippert wrote about how true love *detests* whatever destroys the people we love. "Real love," she said, "stands against the deception, the lie, the sin that destroys … The more a father loves his son, the more he hates in him the drunkard, the liar, the traitor."[1]

German pastor and Christian martyr Dietrich Bonhoeffer expressed something similar when he said, "Nothing can be more compassionate than the severe reprimand which calls another Christian in one's community back from the path of sin."[2]

As leaders, this is an area of Christian discipleship where we can become vulnerable. It is sometimes possible for us to shield ourselves from criticism—even constructive criticism—given by those who are beneath us on the org chart or the family system or the hierarchy of power.

David, ultimately, did not shield himself from hard truths, and this is what made him such a good leader. When Nathan the prophet came to him and called him out for the evil in his life, David did not respond by saying, "Who do you think you are, Nathan? Do you know who it is that you are talking to? Where do you get off …?"

No, David did not resist Nathan's rebuke. Instead, he received it humbly, repented of his sin, and, where possible, made full restitution for it. David's story gives us one of the most comprehensive, historic confessions of sin ever offered:

> Have mercy on me, O God,
> according to your steadfast love;

according to your abundant mercy
 blot out my transgressions.
Wash me thoroughly from my iniquity,
 and cleanse me from my sin!

For I know my transgressions,
 and my sin is ever before me.
Against you, you only, have I sinned
 and done what is evil in your sight....
Behold, you delight in truth in the inward being,
 and you teach me wisdom in the secret
  heart ...

 Wash me, and I shall be whiter than snow....
Hide your face from my sins ...
Create in me a clean heart, O God,
 and renew a right spirit within me.
Cast me not away from your presence,
 and take not your Holy Spirit from me.
Restore to me the joy of your salvation,
 and uphold me with a willing spirit.
   (Psalm 51:1–4, 6–7, 9–12)

But David did not only confess his sin to God. He also turned and confessed his sin to Nathan, saying, "I have sinned against the Lord." Then he turned to Bathsheba, the widowed wife of the soldier he murdered, and became her husband.

Then, in an act of great mercy and kindness, God gave David and Bathsheba a son whose name, Jedidiah, means "beloved of God." This son was also given a second name, Solomon, which means "peace." This gift of a son, born from circumstances involving adultery, murder, and the abuse of power, would later be included in the ancestry of Jesus as a magnificent display of how long, wide, high, and deep the love of God travels:

> David was the father of Solomon by the wife of
> Uriah. (Matthew 1:6)

Matthew went out of his way to include that allusion to the unsavory circumstances surrounding Solomon's birth. He easily could have left out the phrase or said "by Bathsheba" instead of "by the wife of Uriah." Instead, he helps us see how God worked to redeem the sin that David committed and from which he later repented.

As if this weren't enough grace for David, Jesus—the King of all Kings and the true Prince of Peace—would later identify himself as "the son of David" and would call David "a man after God's own heart" (see Acts 13:22).

There are many things we can learn from the life of David. There are many ways that we, as leaders, can look to David as an example and for inspiration. But one of the most important things we *must* learn from him is how essential it is to position ourselves to regularly receive criticism from those around us—especially those who know us best, such as colleagues, friends, and family members—and also to receive it humbly, with gratitude, and with resoluteness to change. Our character must matter more to us than our reputation. We must learn to love the light, even when it exposes the darkness in us, instead of running and hiding from the light.

And this, in spite of his many faults, was where David shined. The aftermath of the Bathsheba scandal presents to us a portrait of greatness—not because David was perfect, but because he was ready and willing to own his imperfection and to do so publicly. His greatness was found in his readiness to humble himself. In this, he shows us one of the key evidences that the Holy Spirit dwells within: a willingness to lose face when he could have easily saved face and a readiness to repent when he *didn't have to* because he was the one holding all the power.

David could have done the same thing to Nathan that he had previously done to Uriah—finish the man off in order to save his own hide and reputation. But he did not. Instead, David chose to listen, humble himself, repent, and seek restoration.

Writer and philosopher Elbert Hubbard wrote, "The final proof of greatness lies in being able to endure criticism without resentment."[3] By this standard, David was a great leader.

Why would David choose repentance over defensiveness and saving face? Better yet, why would we? The answer should be easy. It is for the health of our souls.

Think about it. We welcome the probing and scrutiny of our bodies by doctors. We give them access to our private parts. We say "Yes, of course" when they ask to do an x-ray to evaluate our physical health. We let them probe and prick and cut and

inflict wounds to prevent other, greater wounds from destroying us. Why then would we be any less receptive when it comes
to allowing those closest to us the most intimate access to our
souls and our character? Shouldn't we allow them—even invite
them—to probe, prick, cut, and wound us so that our souls
might be healed?

> Let a righteous man strike me—it is a kindness.
> (Psalm 141:5)

> Faithful are the wounds of a friend. (Proverbs 27:6)

> Whoever brings back a sinner from his wandering
> will save his soul from death. (James 5:20)

Indeed, sometimes bringing out the best in people includes
lovingly exposing the worst in them. *But do we believe this?*

The great civic leader Winston Churchill said that, though
criticism may not be agreeable, it is necessary for all of us. Why?
"Because it fulfills the same function as pain in the human body. It
calls attention to the unhealthy state of things."[4]

Those who resist criticism, especially fair criticism, show themselves to be unhealthy people. Unhealthy people, when criticized,
tend to spin, manipulate, and regroup. True leaders, on the other
hand, confess and repent.

This raises some important questions. What if the criticism
is unfair? What if the critic is someone who doesn't have our best

interest in mind but instead seems to have it out for us, is not worthy of respect, or is saying things about us that are not true? What if the critic, rather than acting out of interest for our health and flourishing, is acting like a pig?

King David can instruct us here, also, in the way that he responds to an irritating man named Shimei. Shimei dislikes how David is leading the people, throws rocks at David, and hurls insults at him, "cursing him continually." David, once again having all the power, could simply kill Shimei on the spot, and one of David's men wants to do just that:

> Abishai the son of Zeruiah said to the king, "Why should this dead dog curse my lord the king? Let me go over and take off his head." But the king said, "… If he is cursing because the LORD has said to him, 'Curse David,' who then shall say, 'Why have you done so?'" (2 Samuel 16:9–10)

Not long ago, Tim Keller posted a tweet that said, "Even if only 20% is true, we can profit from criticism given by people who are badly motivated or whom we don't respect."[5]

Pastor and seminary professor Jack Miller said something similar about certain critiques that he received from detractors—critiques that, in his opinion, were unfair or entirely untrue. Miller professed that whenever somebody would criticize him unfairly or paint a negative caricature of him, he would turn to the person and say, "You don't know the half of it." Being aware of the darkness of his own heart enabled him to regard an unfair criticism as *charitable* compared to the *true* things about him of which his critics were unaware. As Miller famously concluded, "I am much worse than I think I am."

The story is told of the evangelist Dwight L. Moody, who, while preaching the gospel to a large crowd, had his own "Shimei" experience. A young, self-assured, know-it-all seminary student in the crowd began to publicly challenge the things that Moody, the veteran evangelist, was saying. This student rudely interrupted him several times and tried to trip him up. Eventually, Moody got fed up with the young man's rude behavior and snapped at him. The evangelist, widely known as one of the world's most eloquent communicators, used his gift with words to punish the young man, sharply putting him in his place. Thinking that the young man got what he deserved, the crowd showed their hearty approval of Moody's response. Then, later in his talk, Moody stopped himself and said in front of them all:

> Friends, I have to confess before all of you that at the beginning of my meeting I gave a very foolish answer to my brother down here. I ask God to forgive me, and I ask him to forgive me.

Moody demonstrated true leadership and greatness in that moment. Though guilty of the seemingly *lesser* sin, he became the *first* to repent and apologize. He, the one "in power," valued his character and the young man in front of him more than he valued saving face. Though he could have said nothing and gone home satisfied that he had soundly defeated the young antagonist in their public standoff, he instead humbled himself and publicly apologized.

If Jesus, who never committed even the smallest offense, would humble himself and make himself nothing for our sakes; if Jesus would lose face in order to save face for us; if Jesus would allow himself to be exposed, criticized, despised, and rejected in order to cover our shame and prove his great love for us, then it makes sense that we would want to follow in the footsteps of people like Tim Keller, Jack Miller, Dwight L. Moody, and King David by humbling ourselves when *we* are exposed for our shortcomings and sins. For although we are "worse than we think we are," we are also, as Jack Miller also said, "more loved than we ever dared to hope."

Although it is never a good idea to get into a spitting match with an unfair critic who is behaving more like a pig than a Nathan, there are potentially redemptive ways to address her or his "unfairness," should it seem right to do so. I will finish this chapter, then, with a message that I posted on my blog a couple of years ago in response to an unfair and very public criticism that our church received. As you will see, I sought to live in the tension of humbly considering the "20%," while also feeling compelled to protect and defend—but without defensiveness—my faithful friend, who is also, and much more importantly, God's faithful son and servant.

As you read this lengthy letter, watch for the ways in which I tried to take criticism to heart and to articulate—carefully and lovingly, I hope—the reasons why I could not agree with some specific points of criticism.

An Open Letter to a Public Critic

When we decided to do a public forum on same-sex attraction (SSA) at Christ Presbyterian Church, we knew it would involve risk.[6] Any time a church clarifies its approach to matters about which the culture is divided, criticism will come from certain places. Although the public response to our forum with Stephen Moss has been overwhelmingly positive, a handful of concerned parties have gone on social media and blogs and suggested, in some cases quite strongly, that by sharing our platform with a man who lives with SSA (who, significantly, also lives single and chaste in surrender to Jesus), we have somehow been unfaithful to the gospel.

I am responding publicly because of the potential for confusion and unrest if we say nothing. Due to the public nature of the critiques, it seems best, in this instance at least, to respond in a public way. I am protecting the identity of our critics by addressing them collectively as "Friend." I have also chosen this word because it is the nature of a friend to point out concerns. Though we firmly disagree with the concerns that have been expressed, we still appreciate the sharpening that the experience can create. We also appreciate the opportunity it affords, once again, for us to publicly celebrate the broad and tenacious love of Jesus. I pray that somehow in the sharing, those who have heard the critiques of us will understand our heart on the matter ... and more importantly, I pray, the heart of Jesus.

Dear Friend,

What you have called a "refusal to listen" is actually just an inability (not a refusal ... an inability) to agree with you. Knowing that my own heart is capable of deceiving me, I listened very closely and with care to the things you said about us. I just don't see any merit in them. We have opposing views about how to minister to Christians and others living with same-sex attraction.

Would you allow me to begin with a question? You say that the mere presence of SSA is itself sinful and that, because of this, we have no business inviting someone who lives with SSA to speak to our community. Friend, do you believe that there is a difference between temptation and sin? At Gethsemane, Jesus had desires that were contrary to the Father's will—and so he prayed, "Father, take this cup from me."

Father, do I have to die for your will to be accomplished? Papa, I don't want to die. Your will is hard; it goes against my feelings.

It is because of Jesus's courageous "Not my will, but yours be done" that we can say that he was tempted and yet without sin, yes? Can we not say the same of Stephen's SSA—that it is temptation for him, temptation which he has faithfully surrendered to the Father's will?

Say that there are two alcoholics who have been sober for ten years. The first, miraculously, has no cravings for alcohol. The second battles hard against cravings every single day. Does the presence of cravings for the latter make him less faithful than the former? Some would argue, Friend, that he actually might be *more* faithful in his sobriety because, for him, sobriety is a daily fight against the flesh—a fight that he keeps, by the grace of God, *winning*.

If we would not condemn the alcoholic for having cravings, why would we condemn someone who lives with SSA? In the end, how are the two any different? Would we celebrate the sober alcoholic's story as victory but not do the same with the sexually chaste man living with SSA? If Stephen is welcomed into our church's seminary and has faithfully served as staff for our church's campus ministry, do you really feel it is a right, good, excellent, pleasing, and praiseworthy thing in the eyes of Jesus to take us to task on Facebook because we have given him (and the many in our churches whom he represents) a voice?

If you want to know what we think about sex and marriage, may I recommend chapter 8 of my book *Jesus Outside the Lines*? Everything I say in that chapter is congruent with things presented during our recent forum with Stephen. It has openly been our view since my arrival at Christ Presbyterian three years ago. Our view is a public one. It has not been kept in a corner.

As the essay will show, we have always held to a "graciously historic" Christian view of sex and marriage.

And we are thrilled—beyond thrilled actually—to join Jesus in his kind, gentle, patient treatment of "sexually other" men and women. We believe that this kind, gentle, patient treatment is essential and intrinsic to a graciously historic view.

Do you remember how Jesus moved toward the Samaritan woman at the well, then cohabiting with a man who was her fifth sexual partner and also not her husband? *Woman, would you be so kind as to pour me a drink?*

Do you remember the way Jesus showered the woman caught in adultery with assurance? *I do not condemn you.* How wonderful—how unlike a scribe or a Pharisee—for him so boldly and scandalously to establish that he loved her *before* he challenged her on her self- and others-destructive ethics. Grace *and* an invitation to repent are essential, but first things first, right?

It is not our repentance that leads to his kindness but his kindness that leads to our repentance.

Reverse the order of this and you lose Christianity. Reverse the order of this and you lose Jesus. Oh, the horror!

And ... oh, my ... do you remember how Jesus confronted Simon the Pharisee? Remember Simon? Simon, the one who denounced Jesus—can you imagine, denouncing Jesus?—for his warm, receptive disposition toward a sultry-attired prostitute. What was Jesus guilty of? He was *gracing her too much*. The woman comes in uninvited to a dinner party, kisses Jesus's feet with her prostitute's lips, wipes his feet with her prostitute's hair, and anoints him with her prostitute's perfume—*using the tools of her trade* to show love in the only way she knows how. How shocking! How unorthodox! How sexually "other"! And what does Jesus do? He receives it all with joy and then gives her a platform. He points to *her* as the teacher to the teachers. Her lesson? For whoever has the guts to bear it, she puts on a clinic, an in-your-face practicum, on what it means to really worship God.

> Do you see this woman? *This* woman. Learn from her, Simon … learn love from *her*. Learn hospitality from *her*. Learn the scandal of grace from *her*. Learn forgiveness from *her*. Her. Yes, you heard me correctly, Simon. *Her*. She is a person, not a thing. A she, not an it. A masterpiece, not a throwaway. The image of God, not an animal. And I love her much. Do you, Simon? Do you love her much? Do you love her at all?

If Jesus would give such a platform (one that endures to this day) to a woman who *had* succumbed to her unorthodox sexual desires, why would we not give a platform to a man who *has not* succumbed to his?

Friend, we simply disagree. We are so very pleased to associate with Stephen, a faithful Jesus-man, a master of divinity student in our church's seminary, and a future pastor in Jesus's church … *our* church. Stephen, who is saying "No" to his flesh for the sake of Jesus—how courageous! How bold! How faithful! How much Jesus must smile at Stephen, yes? For he is following Jesus in the cruciform way—at a cost that many of us, I daresay most of us, will never quite understand. Yes, Stephen's Christianity *costs* him something. What does following Jesus cost *us*? It's a question worth asking ourselves, yes?

As for the way you have critiqued us, I'm afraid that I do not recognize our motives or behaviors or words or beliefs in the way that you represent them. However, please pray, Friend, that if any of your judgments of us are true, the Lord would reveal it to us and especially to me!

As for an invitation to critique me personally? The answer is … of course, Friend, please critique me as you must and as you will. If it is from God, I would be a fool not to listen and learn from you. By all means, if you can show me where I am unfaithful to Jesus—truly unfaithful to his grace *or* his truth—your rebuke will be as honey on my tongue and new life to my weary, wayward bones. But as it stands, I'm afraid we are simply going to have to disagree regarding your critique. I hope that we can do so agreeably.

Friend, I humbly submit that the more conservative our belief in Jesus, the more liberal our loving will be.

He welcomes sinners and eats with them. When tax collectors, drunks, and gluttons invite him to their parties, he says *yes.* He also says *yes* to smug Pharisees. And to prostitutes. And to cruciform, surrendered, obedient gospel heroes like Stephen Moss.

Friend, if you are convinced that I have a speck in my eye, will you pray that Jesus (if he agrees with you) will graciously remove it? *I will pray the same for you.*

And, Friend, will you believe the gospel for me? *I will believe the same for you.*

Your friend and fellow work in process,

Scott Sauls

Christ Presbyterian Church, Nashville, Tennessee

My sincere hope is that I presented myself as receptive to criticism—prayerfully, thoughtfully open to the possibility that I was in error—while acknowledging that, having examined the public criticism offered, I did not agree with the critique. I also hoped to explain reasonably and clearly why I did not—could not—agree.

My hope is that we all can exhibit humility when faced with criticism—and that we will all stand strong in our convictions and not be afraid to explain them carefully and lovingly.

"When David returned from striking down the Philistine, the women came out of all the cities of Israel, singing and dancing ... And the women sang to one another ... 'Saul has struck down his thousands, and David his tens of thousands.' And Saul was very angry, and this saying displeased him."

1 Samuel 18:6–8

Chapter 4

Envy: A Thorn in the Soul

When we notice ugly things happening in us and the ugliness disturbs us, it's usually a sign that the Holy Spirit is at work. For me, this is good news because I'm disturbed by an ugly thing that often happens in my heart and that needs to be addressed. It's called *envy*.

Experiencing envy is fairly common for leaders and influencers, for those who have "gotten ahead" in life, for those who have "made it to the top" of an organization or a ministry. At its essence, envy is what happens when we compare ourselves with other people and when we covet what they seem to have. When envy is at work, we are comforted when we hear that somebody else is struggling or has failed. Conversely, we feel disturbed when we hear that somebody else is enjoying success or has received an award, a raise, the smallest bit of recognition, or some other positive reward. Envy is the opposite of love because it does not rejoice with those who rejoice or mourn with those who mourn. Instead, envy, in its sick and sinister way, rejoices when others mourn and mourns when others rejoice.

One time I was watching the news and learned that Tom Hanks had fallen off the top 500 celebrities list. Instead of feeling sad for Tom Hanks, I secretly felt glad to hear this news. I rejoiced over those who mourned, so to speak. Why did I feel this way when I heard somebody else's disappointing news? Maybe it was because another's decline in the public eye covers my insecurity about how invisible I feel sometimes. As they say, "Misery loves company." Or maybe it was because it gave me a feeling of superiority over Mr. Hanks; his career was winding down, and mine was just starting to approach its prime.

It's pretty strange, isn't it, that I, a local pastor, would compare myself to a well-known national celebrity? As odd as this is, it is a window into my own twisted and envious heart. Though I am unable to understand why I would have any reason to compare myself to someone who is in an entirely different world—and in an entirely different league than I am—I do understand this: my heart, in being secretly glad about somebody else's sad news, is influenced by envy.

The underlying cause of envy is pride, along with its close cousin, the rival spirit. The rival spirit compels us to say to ourselves, as the Pharisee said in a pep talk to himself that was disguised as a prayer to God, "God, I thank you that *I am not like other men*, extortioners, unjust, adulterers, or even like this tax collector. I fast twice a week; I give tithes of all that I get" (Luke 18:11–12).

Ironically, the Pharisee's boasting is actually a sign of his insecurity, and his inflated ego a sign of his wounded ego.

C. S. Lewis said the following about the rival spirit:

> Pride is essentially competitive … [It] gets no pleasure out of having something, only out of having more of it than the next [person]. We say that people are proud of being rich, or clever, or good-looking, but they are not. They are proud of being richer, or cleverer, or better-looking than others … It's the pleasure of being above all the rest.[1]

It is this kind of "competitive pride" that led to the downfall of King Saul, Israel's first king. After the young shepherd boy David defeated the Philistine giant Goliath with a slingshot and a few stones, all of Israel began to celebrate. According to the story as it is told by Scripture, David was successful in whatever he did because the Lord was with him. His success also pleased the Israelites so much that the women of Israel went public with a celebratory song they had composed about David:

> Saul has struck down his thousands,
>   and David his ten thousands.[2]

Rather than celebrating the young and promising David along with the women, King Saul was angered by the song. He was so furious that he kept a jealous eye on David and thought, *I will pin David to the wall.* And he meant that literally. From that point forward, Saul was *afraid* of and *aggressive* toward David because of the young man's ascending popularity and influence.

As the example of Saul shows us, envy works in all directions. We can envy those who are "up the ladder" or higher in the pecking order than we are, secretly wishing that they would fall from their positions. We can also envy those whose positions are beneath ours, especially when we feel threatened by the attention they receive from their successes. This is why many bosses and supervisors choose not to hire talented people: because talented people, as they develop, have the potential to reach and even surpass the stature of and recognition received by those who employ them.

For similar reasons, senior pastors may pass on opportunities to bring talented young ministers on their teams, bestselling authors and writers may be reluctant to spread the word about talented new authors and writers, or chart-topping musicians may not want to talk about talented new musicians.

Saul has struck down his thousands. By itself, this reads like a supreme compliment. According to the women of Israel, the great King Saul, the mighty warrior-king, had kept Israel safe by single-handedly slaying *thousands* of Israel's enemies. But, following Lewis's point, the moment we add the praise of David to the praise of Saul, "Saul has struck down thousands" suddenly feels more like an insult!

Pride is essentially competitive. It gets no pleasure out of having something, only out of having more of it than the next person. It's the pleasure of being above all the rest.

Or as country music star Gary Allan has said, "You can be the moon and still be jealous of the stars."

I have not been immune to this as a pastor. Ever since I was ordained, I have struggled to avoid comparing myself to other pastors and my ministry to theirs. When I was a church planter working with a core group of fifty people and $100,000, I was jealous of other church planters—especially the ones who graduated from seminary in the same year I did—who had a core group of *seventy* people and *$150,000* to work with. Indeed, I probably would have been envious of a church with a group of fifty-one people and a budget of $100,000.01.

I remember thinking in those early days, *Maybe someday I will be the pastor of a large church with a lot of resources and an ability to influence a lot more people than this.* At least some part of this fantasy had to do with the thought of surpassing my peers. But now, about sixteen years later, I am the senior pastor of a large, growing church with zero debt and a sizable property, and the seeds of envy are still there.

I have come to discover that a pastor with a 3,000-person church can envy the life of a pastor with a 5,000-person church in precisely the same way that a pastor of a 50-person church can envy the pastor of a 70-person church—or even the way the pastor of a 5,000-person church can be envious of the pastor of a 50-person church.

Envy is always lurking. I often want God's kingdom to come on earth as it is in heaven, *but with a caveat*—that his kingdom come *through me* more than it does through others. Because of this, I desperately need to guard my heart, to seek rebuke and grace from Jesus, and to actively and intentionally *pray*, earnestly and often, for those over whom I would be tempted to mourn if they rejoiced or to rejoice if they mourned.

Yes, it's true. We pastors are no different and no less vulnerable to the flesh, the Devil, and the pride of life than other leaders and influencers. Executive leaders, thought leaders, authors, parents, athletes, nonprofit leaders, artists, public servants, entrepreneurs, and pastors … every single one of us has a heart that, apart from the initiative, correction, and affection of Jesus, will be prone to compete and compare.

Have you found this to be true of yourself? Who are the "Davids" in your life who, in comparison to your thousands, have slain ten thousands? Is it difficult for you to see them succeed and receive recognition? Is it difficult for you when you discover that God has given them a bigger staff or a bigger platform, more success or more people applauding them more loudly, or more resources and a more—so it seems—carefree life? Have you enjoyed getting the credit for a thousand slain, only to have your enjoyment spoiled by refrains of ten thousands slain by a person—even a person with a much lower position than yours—whose success and accomplishments draw attention away from yours?

If this is true of you, then it means you are a lot like me. But you are also a lot like the people you envy: their grass never looks as green to them as it does to you. They, too, have hearts that are prone to envy people whose grass *they* think is greener than *theirs*. Those whose span of influence seems greater than yours might envy someone whose span of influence seems greater than theirs. Those who have more resources than you have might envy someone with more resources than they have. Those who have happier and better-adjusted children than you have may envy someone whose children seem happier and better adjusted than theirs. And so it goes.

As Bertrand Russell once said:

> Envy consists in seeing things never in themselves, but only in their relations. If you desire glory, you may envy Napoleon, but Napoleon envied Caesar, Caesar envied Alexander, and Alexander, I daresay, envied Hercules, who never existed.[3]

The British atheist-philosopher's insight is not merely profound; it is also strikingly on point from a biblical perspective. What the Bible calls "selfish ambition," or the quest to achieve greatness and glory for oneself, is a road that leads nowhere. It's a goose chase without a goose. It's a frenetic race to the end of the rainbow only to discover *at* the rainbow's end that there is not, there never was, and there never will be a pot of gold waiting for you there.

Any Saul-like ambition to be the best of the best and the greatest of the great will leave us thirsting for more. This is true *even if we end up winning* and becoming the ones whose lives and situations other people envy.

A couple of years ago, stories about the eighteen-year-old Australian "Instagram star" Essena O'Neill emerged and went viral. By that age, O'Neill had achieved what many young girls would regard as social media world dominance. She had quickly made a career of posting provocative photos and videos of herself online. According to one article, she became an Internet sensation with over half a million Instagram followers and more than 250,000 YouTube subscribers. Her platform had become so significant that, by the time she was eighteen years old, she was able to support herself financially and was offered modeling opportunities in several major cities. Then, with the world at her fingertips (or so it seemed), and at that young age of eighteen, O'Neill announced to her ever-increasing fan base that she had had enough. According to the young sensation, her ascending fame had led her to become less authentic and more miserable because of a growing "addiction to being liked":

> I fell in love with this idea that I could be of value
> to other people. [It was a] snowballing addiction
> to being liked by others ... Yeah 16-year-old
> Essena would have been like "WTF girl you have
> the dream life." So why did I feel so lost, lonely

and miserable? Social media had become my sole identity. I didn't even know who I was without it.[4]

I can't tell you how free I feel without social media. Never again will I let a number define me. IT SUFFOCATED ME. Not because I had 500,000 followers, I felt the same as a young girl, I would just spend hours looking at everyone else's perfect lives and I strived to make mine look just as good ... Guess I succeeded. It's totally stupid.[5]

You might say that, in the world of social media, Essena O'Neill was *winning*. She had slain tens of thousands and had become the envy of multitudes. But, after only two years of fame, Essena O'Neill's own words confirmed that, indeed, Napoleon may envy Caesar, Caesar may envy Alexander, and Alexander may envy Hercules ... but Hercules never existed.

We are not meant to be Hercules. Our souls are not wired for celebrity or for ego-inflating self-advancement. We are not made to stand on pedestals, Rather, we are made to decrease, to *become less*, to make space for *all* the glory and honor and applause to go not to Saul, or even to David, but to the Son of David, who is also the Son of God—King Jesus. We are meant to say, in the words of John the Baptist, "He must increase, but I must decrease" (John 3:30).

What author Ann Voskamp said in response to a blog post by Karen Yates about the odd phenomenon of "Christian celebrity" really says it all:

> [I'm] humbly grateful here for every pastor, teacher, author who sees platform as altar, as a place to come and lay down their lives in utter and complete sacrifice for Christ—knowing that the only platform Christ ever had was a place to come and *die* ... naked and exposed and small and entirely God's ... [We must not turn] a platform given by God to lift high the name of Jesus—into a pedestal praised by men. God alone gave the platform for His name to be exalted, for them to decrease, for man to be invisible and clear glass to God.[6]

I believe that Amy Carmichael, the Protestant missionary to India and orphan advocate, was a beautiful reflection of what Ann wrote about here. After Carmichael died, a loved one went through her collection of photos and discovered that she did not have a single picture of herself. *Not a single selfie.* Every photo was instead a memorial to the good things that God was doing in her world and in the worlds of those whom she loved. Though her platform was, like the platform of Essena O'Neill, quite sizable, Carmichael stewarded her platform for the love and flourishing of others. God had given her a platform for his name to be exalted and for her to decrease, and in this she became an "invisible and clear glass to God."

Business writer Jim Collins calls this the "Level Five Leader." According to Collins, organizations with sustained improvement and growth over fifteen or more years all have this kind of leader, the kind he describes as the *humble CEO*. The Level Five Leader is often described with words like these: quiet, humble, modest, reserved, shy, gracious, mild-mannered, self-effacing, and understated. These leaders didn't believe their own press but were "a paradoxical blend of personal humility and professional will."[7]

Like Amy Carmichael, Level Five Leaders do not have inflated egos, yet they are emotionally full. They are confident, yet they don't exude self-importance. They are more interested in others than they are in getting others interested in them. They have very few selfies yet have hundreds of "pictures" of the people whose livelihoods depend on them and whose flourishing they have undertaken as their personal mission. It is precisely because they *don't* seem interested in drawing attention to themselves that you want to give them your full, undivided attention.

When you are around them, you sense that they are interested in you, that you are important to them, and that they like you. You sense that they are not in it for themselves or for their own glory and advancement but that they're interested in the greater good. They give you confidence that, when it becomes best for the greater good for them to step down and to hand their "throne" over to another leader, they will readily and humbly do so. In Level Five Leaders, we see very little of Saul and a whole lot of Jonathan.

Do you remember Jonathan, the son of Saul and friend of David? This was the young man who, like Ann Voskamp and Amy Carmichael and the Level Five Leaders, learned to overcome envy and the rival spirit through the self-giving act of laying down his life for his friend.

The study of Saul and his son Jonathan is a study of contrast. When the attention of Israel shifted toward David after the Goliath event, when the women started singing songs about how David had slain his ten thousands, Saul wanted to *eliminate* David in order to protect his own stature. In stark contrast, Jonathan wanted to *exalt* David by giving up his own stature.

We are told in 1 Samuel 18 that the soul of Jonathan was knit to the soul of David and that Jonathan loved David as he loved his own soul. We are also told that Jonathan made a *covenant* with David. From that point forward, Jonathan's words and actions toward David revealed a posture of love and loyalty that said, "Come hell or high water, my brother, I am always going to be with you, and I am always going to be for you."

While Saul was jealous *of* David, Jonathan was jealous *for* David. While Saul was ready and eager to sacrifice David's life for his own gain, Jonathan was ready and eager to sacrifice his own life for David's gain.

Now, if anyone had the right to feel threatened by David after the slaying of Goliath, it was Jonathan. Jonathan, after all, was the assumed heir to the throne of his father, Saul. But, knowing from the prophecy of Samuel that God was going to hand the kingdom over to David instead, Jonathan surrendered to God's will for David with the same level of zeal that Jonathan's father, Saul, resisted it.

Wanting to make himself great in comparison to David, Saul became small. Wanting to make himself small in comparison to David, Jonathan became great.

Saul clung desperately to the status of king, and the more he did this, the less of a king he became. Jonathan laid down his right to become king, and the more he did this, the more like a king he became. Although he never ascended to his father's position, Jonathan's faithfulness and character made him a better leader than his father could ever be.

How did Jonathan do this? He took off his robe, his royal garment signifying his royal status, and gave it to David. Then he handed David his sword. In this, Jonathan made himself vulnerable to David because whenever the seat of power transferred from one family to another, the new king would execute each and every descendant of his predecessor. In handing David his sword, Jonathan was saying to his friend, "I will even lay down my life for you that you might ascend to the throne that would otherwise be rightfully mine."

What gave Jonathan the inner resources to do such a thing? I think that, at least in part, it was his memory of something that his father, Saul, had long forgotten:

> As for man, his days are like grass;
> he flourishes like a flower of the field;
> for the wind passes over it, and it is gone,
> and its place knows it no more.

But the steadfast love [literally, the *hesed* or
"covenant love"] of the LORD is from
everlasting to everlasting on those who fear
him. (Psalm 103:15–17)

This raises an important question for those of us in positions
of leadership and influence, we whose hearts are vulnerable to
becoming envious. Can we become free like Jonathan was free? Is
it even possible for us to forsake our "inner Saul" for a better, more
life-giving, and more valiant "inner Jonathan"?

The answer is yes. But to become free, we must first see our envy
of Napoleon and Caesar and Alexander and Hercules—or of David,
or of whomever we are tempted to envy—for what it really is. It is an
exercise in futility. It is a goose chase without a goose.

David and Jonathan are not only powerful but *safe* and
approachable. They are the Level Five types whose photos aren't
dominated by selfies. At their best, they give their lives up for the
flourishing of others, they command attention by not seeking
attention, they become kings by refusing to act like kings, and
they are not boisterous and boastful. Instead, they are quiet, humble, modest, reserved, shy, gracious, mild-mannered, self-effacing,
and understated. In addition, they do not believe their own press,
and they have a paradoxical blend of personal humility and professional will.

David and Jonathan are men who have encountered and lived
their lives before the face of the greater King and the greater Friend
Yahweh, the Covenant King and Lord of all.

Later in history, Jesus, "great David's greater Son," would come into the world as Yahweh in human form. Jesus became the King who conquered by making himself small and the Friend who sticks closer than a brother and who, because of a covenant, lays down his life for the sake of his friends.

King Jesus, whose kingdom is forever and whose government will always increase, who looks at every square inch of his universe and declares, "Mine,"[8] won this right by sacrificing himself. He gained exaltation by taking the low position. Jesus, the Prince of Peace, took off his royal robe and placed it upon us. He handed us his sword, making himself vulnerable to us, and we used it against him. But he did not strike back. Instead, he did nothing out of rivalry or conceit—but in humility counted us more significant than himself, looking not to his own interests but to the great need of a humanity dying from a fixation on itself. Though the rightful heir to the throne, Jesus made himself nothing, set aside his glory, and became obedient to death on a cross … all to secure our flourishing.

When this kind of love is offered to us, why would we feel a need, ever again, to compete and compare? Why would we feel any need, ever again, to make ourselves great?

Because Hercules? He never existed.

"When I look at your heavens, the work of your fingers, the moon and the stars, which you have set in place, what is man that you are mindful of him, and the son of man that you care for him? Yet you have made him a little lower than the heavenly beings and crowned him with glory and honor. You have given him dominion over the works of your hands; you have put all things under his feet."

Psalm 8:3–6

Chapter 5

Insecurity: Growing Big from Feeling Small

Today, a search online for books about "religion" and "spirituality" will reveal a selection of something close to 1.5 million books.

The pervasive writing of and demand for religious and spiritual works reveals an inner thirst that has not been adequately quenched. Whatever our stories, our experiences, our people, our place, and our values might be, we are all in varying degrees searching for a sustained inner poise and equilibrium that we have not yet experienced. This inner dissatisfaction, this primal insecurity with ourselves and about ourselves, is reflected artfully in a now-famous lyric from the Irish rock band U2:

I believe in the Kingdom come
Then all the colors will bleed into one, bleed
        into one
But yes I'm still running.
You broke the bonds and you loosened the
        chains
You carried the cross of my shame, oh my shame
You know I believe it
But I still haven't found what I'm looking for.[1]

Clearly, this particular lyric is addressed to Jesus, the very One who carried the cross of our shame. Here, Bono and crew (most in the band identify as Christian) write and sing as those who are convinced of a greater fame and a greater influence than their own—of Jesus Christ, who has died, who has risen, and who will come again. They write and sing as those who anticipate a new world in which there will be no more suffering or confusion or sorrow. Their belief is based on a saving narrative in which the Creator broke the bonds of slavery to sin and self, loosened the chains of injustice, and covered the shame of all the shameful things we are prone to deny and hide. Yet even believing these things and living their lives from an enormous platform, there's still this nagging sense of not having found what they're looking for.

Can you relate to the lyric? Can you relate to the cry for release that resides beneath it? Can you *feel* the tension of the "already" and the "not yet"? Can you identify, perhaps, with being on top of the world in the eyes of many while still feeling insecure about your place in the world? Most would agree that the lyric reveals, even painfully so, that the quest for inner poise and equilibrium, the quest for the security of having been made *complete*, is a quest for all human beings, whether they believe in God or not.

For leaders and influencers, this inner conflict is especially common. As a leader, I am painfully in touch with my own restlessness, especially in the context of my work and goals. Though some would look at my work and label it as some sort of "success," the truth is that—even in my best and smoothest seasons of leading, when momentum is there and goals are being reached and a mission is being accomplished—the disequilibrium is still there.

My most common prayer request these days is that God would give me consistent, uninterrupted sleep, because in the middle of almost every night, I lie awake for two to four hours wrestling. I wrestle with preoccupation, with self-doubt, with the dissatisfaction of unmet expectations and unrealized goals and dreams, with pressure that I put on myself or that I fear others will put on me, with the burdens of the day behind me and the day ahead of me, and with the sense that my work is never going to be satisfactory or complete. In other words, I wrestle over the unique calling of leadership—which is both an unspeakable privilege and a burden that must be carried, often alone.

Because the world is quiet in the middle of the night without the usual distractions of checklists, schedules, deadlines, meetings, interruptions and screens and iThings, I also find myself wrestling with an inner *dis*equilibrium in relation to God.

For me, the presence of God is most palpable when the world is quiet. But the presence of God is not always comforting to me. Sometimes being in the presence of God, or just thinking about God in the middle of the night, is disorienting and disruptive. There are few things like the presence of God that remind me that I am not yet what I am meant to be; that I fall short of the mark; that I am more small than I am significant; that, one hundred years from now, my name will be forgotten by the weary world in which I now live. I will die, and the world will move on. Even in my own church, a hundred years from now, its members will have never heard of me. It is quite possible that not even my own great-great-grandchildren will know my name or care what I accomplished.

Yes, my heart makes noise. My inner life is a paradox of comfort and accusation, inner rest and inner restlessness, enjoyment of God's grace and despair at my own lack of grace, awareness of my completion in Christ and knowledge of feeling incomplete. Added to this, and related to my calling to lead, you'll find a feeling of simultaneous momentum and failure. In the middle of the night especially, God is my refuge on one hand, and the darkness is my companion on the other. In the presence of God and in the quiet, most of my anxieties and worries and self-loathing and guilt rise to the surface. And, if I'm being honest, in the middle of the night, the words of Jesus often fail me. Or, more accurately said, my heart fails the words of Jesus:

> Come to me, all who labor and are heavy laden, and
> I will give you rest. Take my yoke upon you, and

learn from me, for I am gentle and lowly in heart, and you will find rest for your souls. For my yoke is easy, and my burden is light. (Matthew 11:28–30)

For me, the yoke sometimes feels hard, and the burden sometimes feels heavy. And the single thing that comes between my heart and the easy yoke and the light burden ... is *me*. I relate to these words from Brennan Manning, the deceased Roman Catholic who, in many ways, still teaches me so much about grace:

When I get honest, I admit I am a bundle of paradoxes. I believe and I doubt, I hope and get discouraged, I love and I hate, I feel bad about feeling good, I feel guilty about not feeling guilty. I am trusting and suspicious. I am honest and I still play games. Aristotle said I am a rational animal; I say I am an angel with an incredible capacity for beer.[2]

It is for such honest and raw statements that I have always been fond of Brennan Manning. And like Manning, I am a bundle of paradoxes. His words give me hope about my restless thoughts that come in the middle of the night. Not only this, they remind me of something that the German theologian Rudolph Otto said about people in the Bible when they came into the presence of God—namely, that the experience of God's presence was disturbing, perilous, traumatic, and dangerous. Or, as Lewis wrote about Narnia's Aslan, he is good—but he is not safe.[3]

In the Bible, there's a story that especially helps me feel okay about not yet having fully found what I'm looking for. This particular story is about Jacob, the ancient patriarch of Israel, when he lay awake in the middle of the night wrestling with God. To my comfort, the Jacob story confirms that wrestling in the middle of the night—experiencing disequilibrium and restless thoughts and self-doubt and insomnia and an overall disposition of *insecurity*—might be more a sign of spiritual *vitality* than it is a sign of being spiritually lost. It might be more a sign of being spiritually *full* than it is a sign of being spiritually empty. The Jacob story also gives me hope that when I am wrestling and feeling disoriented and insecure, God could be more *near* than he is far away.

The Jacob story—specifically the part about *his* insecurity and wrestling—is recorded in Genesis 32:22–32. Jacob, the son of Isaac, was left to do battle in the presence of God while alone in the dark. We might call it Jacob's "dark night of the soul." All of his life, Jacob had been haunted by an endless search to hear a blessing said over him, one spoken not by a small and insignificant voice but by a strong and authoritative one, a voice that would say to his soul, "You are okay, Jacob. You are noticed. You are loved. You are *liked and enjoyed*. You have value. You matter."

In Jacob, we see a characteristic that most leaders and influencers share: Jacob is *driven*. And the trait is one that our similarly driven contemporaries share. One wonders if, during his dark night, Jacob was haunted by the same thoughts that have haunted pop singer Madonna all of her life:

I have so many [regrets] ... and I have none. I wish I hadn't done a lot of things, but, on the other hand, if I hadn't I wouldn't be here. But, then again, nobody works the way I work. I have an iron will. And all of my will has always been to conquer some horrible feeling of inadequacy. I'm always struggling with that fear. I push past one spell of it and discover myself as a special human being and then I get to another stage and think I'm mediocre and uninteresting. And I find a way to get myself out of that. Again and again. My drive in life is from this horrible fear of being mediocre. And that's always pushing me, pushing me. Because even though I've become Somebody. I still have to prove that Somebody. My struggle has never ended and it probably never will.[4]

Like Madonna, Jacob had been driven by insecurity, by the horrible fear of going unnoticed, of being thought insignificant, of looking back on his life having been labeled a Nobody instead of a Somebody in the eyes of the world, in the eyes of God, and in his own eyes.

In Madonna's case, the drive and insecurity and fear of not being treated as Somebody remain with her in spite of great success that spans three decades. Even in her sixties, she is still one of the world's most celebrated pop stars. Yet, in her own words, her struggle has never ended, and it probably never will.

One of the privileges I enjoy as a pastor in Nashville is that I get to serve as chaplain to several musicians and bands. Six evenings of the year, I offer a short teaching and prayer for a handful of artists at Nashville's historic Ryman Auditorium. The experience also includes interacting backstage with the artists. Recently, I caught about ten minutes with a woman whose name and music you would easily recognize. Like Madonna, she has enjoyed—and apparently also suffered from—being a celebrated artist and influencer.

During our conversation, I asked her what it was like to be her. Specifically, I asked her what it was like to have such a large platform for her music, so many adoring fans, and so much opportunity to influence others.

She paused for a moment and then said, "Do you really want to know what it's like to be me? Can I answer you honestly? Okay then. Here goes. Night after night, I fill arenas and stadiums. Night after night, I have thousands of adoring fans eating out of the palm of my hand. In just five minutes, I will step out on the historic Ryman stage and relive this experience once again, and again tomorrow in another auditorium and in another city, and again the next night and then the night after that. And, from the moment I step foot on the stage until I walk backstage again, I am the loneliest person in the room."

This musician's transparent response to me underscored what Bono and Madonna and also Saint Augustine have underscored as well: Our hearts are going to be insecure until they find their security in God. Our hearts are going to be restless until they find their rest in him. No amount of applause or praise or year-end bonuses or "attaboys" or "attagirls" from other people will satisfy the ache and help us to find what we're looking for. Only the strong, authoritative voice of God can do that.

As for Jacob, his insecurity had haunted him from infancy. Jacob was a twin, the second-born son of Isaac. From the earliest days of childhood, Jacob had lived with the pain of knowing that he was his father's *second* favorite son. Isaac, as the Bible tells us, loved Jacob's twin brother, Esau, more. And Isaac's years of doting on and favoring Esau had wounded Jacob deeply.

There is another significant detail about Jacob's childhood. His father named him "Jacob," a name that in Hebrew means "liar." Can you imagine growing up with a name like this … with a name that served as a painful reminder that ever since your birth, your own father pronounced a curse over you instead of a blessing? Your own father, from your earliest days, looked upon you with contempt instead of favor. Your own father, from your earliest days, decided that, as far as he was concerned, you were going to be a Nobody instead of a Somebody.

Jacob resorted to desperate measures in an attempt to reverse the negative verdict spoken over him by Isaac. When he and his brother, Esau, were adult men and Isaac had lost his eyesight and was dying, Jacob went in to his father posing as Esau. "Father, it's me, Esau," Jacob said. "Give me my blessing." And then, believing that the son of his scorn was instead son of his love, Isaac spoke the blessing—unaware and under false pretense—over Jacob instead of Esau.

Some have said that Jacob's deceit was the first recorded case of identity theft.[5] But what was Jacob's motivation? Why, under false pretense and knowing that it would not be long before both Isaac and Esau would find him out, did Jacob deceive anyway? Ten out of ten therapists would say that it was because Jacob, like every other child in the world, craved a paternal blessing. More than anything, he longed to hear words of affirmation spoken over him by his father. And if the blessing can only be gained under false pretenses, a child will resort to any measure to satisfy this primal craving. Simply put, Jacob wanted more than anything to hear from his father's lips, "I see you. You matter. I love you. I *like* you. You matter to me."

My own children have sought similar blessings from me. For example, when our youngest daughter, Ellie, was six years old, she asked me one time to sit and watch her while she read a book. *Silently.* So I sat there in the quiet for about thirty minutes, watching her read. And then I gave her what she was looking for. "Way to go, Ellie! I am so proud of you! You read so well! I really enjoyed watching you read!" And I did.

What is it in the heart of a child that makes her or him long to be watched and to be seen, even while doing something so mundane, something so unspectacular as reading a book to herself quietly? It's the same thing that resides in the heart of a grown-up, including leaders and influencers like Bono, Madonna, my friend from backstage at the Ryman, Jacob, and me. In the heart of every child, in the heart of every adult, in the heart of every leader and influencer resides the longing to be watched and then to be praised, to be known and then to be loved, to be seen and exposed and then not to be rejected. It's a longing to be approved and favored. It's a longing to be Somebody in the eyes of a greater Somebody. It's a longing to be secure.

Comedian and talk-show host Ellen DeGeneres speaks about a fictitious "approval patch" that she wears under her sleeve every day. The approval patch, she says, works just like a nicotine patch. Throughout the day, it releases small doses of approval … and she can't rip it off her arm until the craving stops.

But for Ellen, Jacob, and the rest of us, the craving never stops. We are made in the image of God, the very purpose of whose existence is to be glorified and adored and given honor and praise. Why, then, would we ever think it odd to desire praise ourselves, being made in his image?

There's a Groucho Marx skit that I love because I relate to it so much. In the skit, Groucho is having a conversation with a friend, in which he goes on and on (and on and on …) about himself. In the course of his continual chatter about himself, he slips into a brief moment of self-awareness and apologizes to his friend for talking so much about himself. He politely says to his friend, "Well. Enough about me. Let's talk about you. What do *you* think about me?"

Aren't we all wearing the approval patch? This is why so many of us pursued positions of leadership and influence in the first place. Isn't it because—or at least in part because—we crave those daily, constant, small but significant doses of approval seeping into our systems … every minute of the hour, every hour of the day, every day of the week, every week of the month, and every month of the year?

And we can't rip it off until the craving stops. This is why we get nervous when a board member emails us and the subject line reads, "Can we talk?" This is why, even on the heels of a great year, something inside us dreads an upcoming review of our work. This is why we feel threatened by talented up-and-comers in our industries and organizations and ministries, and why we lie awake at night wrestling with our inner Jacob and wrestling with God. We think, *My struggle has never ended and it probably never will.*

By the time we get to Genesis 32, Jacob is a broken man. God has chosen him to be the father and leader of the twelve tribes of Israel—the kingly figure of a family of twelve sons whose "tribes" will eventually establish an entire nation. Therefore, it is critical that the wounded Jacob undergo healing. For this to happen, and for Jacob to be able to release the wounds of the years of cursing and neglect from his father, he has to go through a dark night of the soul. He has to wrestle with the presence of God—the same God who put him in a family with a dad who named him *Liar*.

We are told that Jacob was alone all night, wrestling with God until daybreak. Now, if you know anything about wrestling, you know that even three minutes on the mat with an opponent is exhausting. But Jacob, we are told, wrestled with God until daybreak … the whole night long! At dawn, God said to him, "Let me go," to which the exhausted yet resilient Jacob replied, "I won't let you go until you bless me."

I won't let go until *you* bless me. Until *God* blesses me. Until the Supreme *Somebody* affirms that I, Jacob, am going to be treated as a loved one instead of a liar, as a favored son instead of a contemptible throwaway, as a Somebody instead of a Nobody.

And it was there on the ground, wrestling with God from evening until daybreak, that Jacob finally found what he was looking for. There on the ground, he heard the voice of a Father who had loved him since before he was born, who had declared that he, Jacob "the younger," would rule over his older brother, Esau, as the favored son. Jacob heard a Father who was not blind but who could see him clearly all the way down to his core, conveying to him something similar to the words that would one day be uttered to an even greater Son:

"You are my beloved Son; with you I am well pleased" (Mark 1:11).

Approval patch no longer necessary. Ceaseless striving for recognition and applause no longer required. No more fear of mediocrity or of your legacy being forgotten. Because now, Jacob, I am giving you a new name. From now on, you will be named *Israel*, which means "he wrestles with God."

When you've wrestled with God and prevailed with a blessing, it has a way of breaking the spell of insecurity and fear. It has a way of making you less needy for approval and applause and, therefore, more poised to love and to serve—which is precisely what a leader and influencer is meant to do.

Recently, a friend sent me a YouTube video of a magnificent conversation between Bono and Eugene Peterson about the Psalms. The conversation had first been initiated by Bono, who had read some of Peterson's books and wanted to meet him. Initially, Peterson declined the request to meet because he was in the middle of translating the book of Isaiah for what has now become *The Message*, a contemporary paraphrase of the Bible.

In the video, there is an interview of Eugene Peterson where the interviewer expresses shock that the pastor and writer would turn down a meeting with the world-famous rock star for *any* reason. Speculating that this could have been the first time anyone ever turned down a meeting with Bono, the interviewer said, "This is *Bono* we're talking about, for goodness' sakes!"

Eugene Peterson humbly (and humorously) responded to the interviewer, "But this is *Isaiah* we're talking about."

We actually *are* already Somebodies who have received blessing and favor from a Father in heaven who is not blind but who sees us all the way to our core. We have been affectionately named and are so secure in our Father's love that we are free even to turn down a meeting request from a world-famous rock star. Put another way, the love of God, when taken hold of, frees us from any need to be noticed, to make a name for ourselves, to find significance through achievement and advancement or from leading and influencing others. We already *have* these bene-dictions and blessings—and in infinite supply—from the Father who is not blind to our value but who sees us and loves us just the same!

What struck me most from the video of Bono and Eugene Peterson was how free Peterson was to relate to Bono as a valued fellow carrier of the image of God and fellow wrestler, instead of relating to him as an untouchable world-famous rock star. Because Peterson was secure in the Father's blessing, he did not *need* Bono's company or approval. He did not *need* for the rest of the world to know that he, Eugene Peterson, had been sought out for friendship by a world-famous rock star. There were no selfies that followed with the caption "Hanging out at my house with my good friend Bono" or even the hashtag #BonoAndMe. No, just a quiet conversation in the woods of Montana. Secure in the blessing and favor of the Wrestler who sees him, Peterson was free to simply love and listen to the man in front of him like a brother. The man happened to be a world-famous rock star, but even more than that, the man was a fellow Somebody who, like Eugene Peterson, also had the spell of fame broken by the bigger, better blessing of the Supreme *Somebody*.

I believe that the key phrase in Jacob's wrestling story is the one in which he said to God, "I won't let *you* go." In order to tighten his grip on the blessing of God, Jacob had to loosen and even let go of the grip he previously had on achieving the blessing of his father, Isaac. And so it was in tightening his grip on the God who had always had a grip on him that Jacob finally found what he was looking for. Although he left the wrestling match with a permanent limp, he walked away as a man who was finally free—in the words of Eugene Peterson—to "run with the horses."[6]

Jacob finally found what he was looking for, not in spite of his dark night of the soul, but because of it. In finding what he was looking for, he was now poised to love and serve—which is precisely what a leader and influencer is meant to do.

The point is this: *fear God and you'll never have to be afraid of anything.*

Once you begin to fear God—that is, once you start ascribing supreme significance to *his* pronouncements over you versus all of the more fragile and fading pronouncements coming from other lesser, fragile, finite, fading voices—you'll be free to look outside of yourself and to start loving and serving. The very last words of Jesus's life, "It is finished," are also the very *first* words that your Father in heaven has pronounced over you. When you realize that, these words of King David can also become your theme song:

> The LORD is my light and my salvation;
>   whom shall I fear?
> The LORD is the stronghold of my life;
>   of whom shall I be afraid? …
>
> Cast me not off; forsake me not,
>   O God of my salvation!
> For my father and my mother have forsaken me,
>   but the LORD will take me in.
>   (Psalm 27:1, 9–10)

It seemed that Bono found what he was looking for in the woods of Montana with Eugene Peterson. But Peterson was not the answer for Bono as much as he was a gateway *to* the answer. For Eugene Peterson and Bono, Jesus is the answer to the insecurity and restlessness and the dark nights of the soul.

Jesus is the true Jacob and the true father and king of the tribes of Israel.

Jesus is also the wrestler of whom Jacob is merely a shadow. Jesus is the forsaken Son who wrestled with God, but instead of prevailing, he lost. Whereas Jacob was given a limp, Jesus was put in the grave after *his* dark night of the soul.

On the cross, Jesus lost the Father's blessing and received a curse so that we, who have all our lives lived beneath a curse, could receive the Father's blessing. On his way to the cross, Jesus released his grip on the Father and cried "Not my will, but yours be done" so that the Father could forever tighten his grip on us. On the cross, Jesus, who is the firstborn of all creation, gave up his birthright so he could pass it on to us, so that we could find what we have been looking for. Because of this great love of Jesus, we are now free to choose an encounter with Isaiah over an encounter with a world-famous rock star.

Isaiah, the one whom Eugene Peterson preferred over even Bono, reminds us of the Father's blessing to the tribes of Israel— and also to us—with hopeful, healing words:

> You shall be a crown of beauty in the hand of the
>   LORD,
>   and a royal diadem in the hand of your God.
> You shall no more be termed Forsaken,
>   and your land shall no more be termed
>   Desolate,
> but you shall be called My Delight Is in Her,
>   and your land Married;
> for the LORD delights in you,
>   and your land shall be married.

For as a young man marries a young woman,
    so shall your sons marry you,
and as the bridegroom rejoices over the bride,
    so shall your God rejoice over you.
        (Isaiah 62:3–5)

"A person who has toiled with wisdom and knowledge and skill must leave everything to be enjoyed by someone who did not toil for it. This also is vanity and a great evil. What has a man from all the toil and striving of heart with which he toils beneath the sun? For all his days are full of sorrow, and his work is a vexation. Even in the night his heart does not rest. This also is vanity."

Ecclesiastes 2:21–23

Chapter 6

Anticlimax: A Gateway to Hope

Like many top leaders, the ancient writer of Ecclesiastes had succeeded by virtually every earthly measure. He had created great works, built magnificent houses, planted fruitful vineyards, and made beautiful parks. He had a large staff working for him and great possessions, herds, flocks, silver, gold, and treasure (Ecclesiastes 2:4–11). The ancient writer was a picture of a self-made man, of a businessman and leader who had "made it," and whose dreams had been fulfilled to the uttermost.

Yet, in spite of such great success, he described his experience of success as one of *vexation*. To be vexed is to be bothered, annoyed, irritated. Shakespeare used a form of the term at the beginning of *A Midsummer Night's Dream* to describe a father who was intensely troubled by his daughter: "Full of vexation come I, with complaint / Against my child, my daughter Hermia." Vexation is severe distress—as the writer of Ecclesiastes used the word, he hated life, he lived in despair, and he saw everything about his life, including his success, as empty and vain (Ecclesiastes 2:17–26).

The writer was simply telling the truth about life in a fallen world—namely, that we can give our lives to a vision or set of goals, end up achieving them, and still be unsatisfied. Very common to the human experience is the feeling that nothing, ultimately, will satisfy the longings we have. In a very real sense, the best we can hope for is an ability to enjoy some of our successes and, in the end, to die. Perhaps it's partly the looming reality of death that spoils our enjoyment of even our greatest accomplishments and successes.

A recent edition of *Business Insider* reported that Markus Persson, the thirty-six-year-old founder and president of Minecraft, sold the company for a whopping $2.5 billion. Following the sale, he purchased a $70 million mansion and spent his days "living the dream" with lavish parties, high-end vacations and world travel, and making friends with famous celebrities.

At the peak of his success, when those looking at his life from the outside might assume he was one of the happiest, most fulfilled people in the world, Persson sent out two reflections on Twitter that told a very different story:

> The problem with getting everything is you run
> out of reasons to keep trying.

Hanging out with a bunch of friends and
partying with famous people, able to do whatever
I want, and I have never felt more isolated.[1]

Similarly, a friend recently sent me an essay about the Silicon
Valley work culture. In the essay, the writer, who had interfaced
over a period of time with several young, successful entrepreneurs
and cutting-edge business leaders, concluded that, while Silicon
Valley may be awash in material wealth, its inhabitants are still
afflicted with poverty. Rather than being materially poor, many
of these Silicon Valley leaders experience a poverty that is chiefly
relational, spiritual, and emotional.

This is the anticlimax of success. It is the disillusionment of
those who have worked all their lives to get to the top and who,
once they finally "arrive," experience major letdown. Theirs is the
story of chasing the pot of gold at the end of the rainbow only to
discover a pile of sticks instead.

For many, like the writer of Ecclesiastes with all of his worldly
success, the inner life gets infected by vexation, vanity, a chasing
after the wind. Anticlimax afflicts us with a feeling of letdown—
and even despair—over the false promise made by the dream of
making it to the top. It's the promise that position and power and
money and fame will end up being the things that fill our souls.
As with Trent Reznor from the nihilist band Nine Inch Nails, anticlimax leads the disenchanted soul to renounce success and say,
"You can have it all, my empire of dirt." In the end, says Reznor,
such so-called empires will let us down and make us hurt because

the empires fail to deliver on the taste of heaven that they so often promise to us.[2]

When I was in seminary, one of my professors told our class of future pastors that we should not expect to have close friends in the churches we lead. It is always best, the professor said, to seek out friendships with people who are *not* part of our church families.

I found this professor's advice not only strange but also offensive. How in the world am I supposed to shepherd a church to live in community with one another while not myself living in community *with* them? Furthermore, what are we to make of how the apostle Paul got so close to the members of the church at Ephesus that there was uncontrollable weeping by everybody, including Paul, when it came time for him to move on to another city to plant another church? What are we to make of how the members of that church sent their pastor off with warm embraces and kisses (Acts 20:13–37)? And what are we to make of how Jesus, the prototypical Pastor himself, spent virtually every day living alongside, eating with, serving, and self-disclosing with his tribe of twelve disciples and, even more deeply, with his inner ring of three friends, Peter, James, and John?

Having now served for nineteen years in pastoral ministry, I still resist the professor's advice that pastors should seek their primary community *outside* of their own church communities. I remain committed to this and can safely say that my closest friends *are* from the church in which I serve as pastor ... and they always have been in previous churches I have served as well.

Yet from a practical and experiential standpoint, I understand why the professor would advise us in this way. In every church we have served, Patti and I have experienced rejection from people in the church who had, for a time, been our close friends. The reasons have been many for these "friend breakups." Sometimes the breakup occurred because I, as pastor, was not doing enough to give these friends the kind of church they wanted—a better youth or children's ministry, different music, a different style of preaching, or a different vision than what I was offering to them. At other times, the breakup happened because of a false narrative about me, from gossip and mischaracterizations that put me in a negative light. And, at still other times, a breakup would happen because the negative gossip about me was not false but true … that is, it happened because of some real flaw or shortcoming in me that friends decided they didn't want to deal with anymore.

Even though we have had four or five of these heartbreaking experiences with members or staff of the churches I have led, we are still inclined to pursue our deepest friendships from *inside* our church community, if for no other reason that what C. S. Lewis said in a book he wrote as his wife, Joy, was dying from cancer:

> To love at all is to be vulnerable. Love anything
> and your heart will be wrung and possibly broken. If you want to make sure of keeping it intact
> you must give it to no one, not even an animal.
> Wrap it carefully round with hobbies and little

luxuries; avoid all entanglements. Lock it up safe
in the casket or coffin of your selfishness. But in
that casket, safe, dark, motionless, airless, it will
change. It will not be broken; it will become
unbreakable, impenetrable, irredeemable. To love
is to be vulnerable.[3]

If you are a leader, my guess is that you have experienced similar types of relational anticlimax in the group, team, company,
network, or association you have been given to lead. There have
likely been other letdowns for you as well.

The 1999 movie *Office Space* features a character named
Peter. He, while processing his work-related boredom, cynicism,
and depression in the office of a hypnotherapist, provides this
admission:

So I was sitting in my cubicle today and I realized, ever since I started working, every single day
of my life has been worse than the day before it.
So that means that every single day that you see
me, that's the worst day of my life … I'd say that
in a given week I probably only do about fifteen
minutes of real, actual work.[4]

Peter's experience, though told from the perspective of a man
stuck as a cog in the wheel in the middle of his company's org
chart, also mirrors the emotional reality of leaders. We get into a

job, we put our hearts and souls and guts into a vision, and along the way, we grow disillusioned.

For us pastors, anticlimax can take many forms. In spite of our best efforts and most faithful prayers and shepherding and preaching, the popular church down the street *still* attracts some of our members. In spite of the comprehensive, compassionate, and costly care given to a hurting church member, he says that he feels uncared for by the church and then leaves in a huff. In spite of counseling a couple for two years in hopes that their struggling marriage will heal, they get a divorce. In spite of putting hours of study and preparation into preaching, three emails arrive on Monday telling you how disappointing, offensive, or theologically imprecise your sermon was. In spite of putting in your best effort to craft worship services that artfully draw people into the presence of God, the varied criticisms still come: the liturgy is too formal *and* too informal; the music is too upbeat *and* too mellow; the song selection is too contemporary *and* too traditional; the people are not welcoming enough *and* too invasive. In spite of spending countless hours of prayer that God would bring revival and renewal to your church, the church remains stunted in its growth, mundane in its ministry, lukewarm in its love, invisible in its impact, and held back by the demands and drama of its most narcissistic and divisive members. Or so it seems.

In my own moments of pastoral discouragement and isolation, I have often forced myself to remember that Jesus Christ—who was not an imperfect leader like me, but a *perfect* one—faithfully and prayerfully poured everything he had into his twelve disciples for a solid three years. And what was his return on his investment? Judas betrayed him for a handful of coins, Peter denied him three times, his three closest friends fell asleep when he asked them for prayer, and at the moment when he needed them most, they all abandoned him and left him to die alone. How must Jesus, the Author and Perfecter of our faith, have felt each time he referred to his closest friends as "you who are of little faith"?

As if this weren't anticlimactic enough, Jesus had only 120 followers *after* he rose from the dead (Acts 1:15).

If the King of all Kings, the Governor of all Governors, the Boss of all Bosses, and the Leader of all Leaders—who did everything in perfection and was so "successful" in his mission that he even conquered death—would undergo anticlimax, then we should certainly expect the same for ourselves.

In addition to being deeply frustrating, this is also strangely comforting. When the company goes bankrupt, when the critics write a scathing review, when, after studying for days, we get a C minus on the exam, when the surgery ends with a corpse instead of renewed vitality, when the athletic training produces a crippling injury instead of a medal, when the restaurant goes belly up, when the launch is less than spectacular, when the competition drowns us, when our children reject the beliefs and values we have instilled in them for years, when the sermon or blog post gets fifteen criticisms and zero thank-yous, when the church doors have to close … Yes, whenever and wherever there is anticlimax, we can remind ourselves that *Jesus went first*. We can take solace in this:

> For we do not have a high priest who is unable
> to sympathize with our weaknesses, but one who
> in every respect has been tempted as we are, yet
> without sin. (Hebrews 4:15)

Christian writer Frederick Buechner once wrote that the kind of work God usually calls us to is the kind of work that we need most to do and that the world most needs to have done. Buechner concluded that the place God calls us to is the place where our deep gladness and the world's deep hunger meet.

Yet we know that, in many instances, Buechner's theory about calling is precisely that: *a theory*. Even in the best and most influential roles of leadership, what is supposed to be "deep gladness" for the leader can wind up feeling empty instead. Perhaps this is why a recent world Gallup Poll revealed that what the world wants most—even more than food, shelter, safety, and peace—is a satisfying job.[5] This longing experienced by people all over the world is connected to something that was revealed in another poll: namely, that 87 percent of workers feel disengaged and dissatisfied in the jobs they *do* have.[6]

What are we to do with this painful reality? Where are we to go with it? I believe that there are two forerunners of our faith—one from the Old Testament and one from the New Testament—whose perspectives can help us immensely.

The first forerunner is the prophet Isaiah. Isaiah was a faithful man of God and a messenger to the people of Israel, and he was so despised for his faithful preaching that, according to historians, he was sawed in two. Listen to God's initial call on Isaiah's life, and consider Buechner's words about calling. While it is easy to discern the "deep hunger" in Isaiah's story, it is not easy to understand *how* the prophet could experience "deep gladness" with a calling like this:

> [The Lord] said, "Go, and say to this people:
>
> "'Keep on hearing, but do not understand;
> keep on seeing, but do not perceive.'
> Make the heart of this people dull,
>   and their ears heavy,
>   and blind their eyes;
> lest they see with their eyes,
>   and hear with their ears,
> and understand with their hearts,
>   and turn and be healed."
> Then I said, "How long, O Lord?"
> And he said:
> "Until cities lie waste
>   without inhabitant,
> and houses without people,
>   and the land is a desolate waste,
> and the LORD removes people far away,

and the forsaken places are many in the

midst of the land." (Isaiah 6:9–12)

Isaiah was given a dismal picture of his future, a sorrowful and hurtful experience of leading others, and a depressing prediction of loss, failure, rejection, and anticlimax. How could he respond "Here am I; send me!" to *this* call? How could Isaiah think it possible for his own *deep gladness* to somehow be drawn out through the sorrow and deep hunger of an anticlimactic experience of leading?

The second forerunner is the apostle Paul, a man who had tasted what it was like to achieve the equivalent of an Ivy League degree, to run in elite circles, and to advance in his career far beyond his rabbi peers. Yet, once he bowed the knee to Jesus, Paul lost the status and recognition that he had grown so accustomed to in his Jewish circles. Like Isaiah, he would be mistreated because of his faithfulness and rejected because of his faith. Paul was persecuted, struck down, beaten, abandoned, and imprisoned as a direct by-product of *leading* in the name of Christ.

Yet, from a prison cell, Paul and his quill and parchments gave birth to a letter that is known by Bible scholars as *the Epistle of Joy*—what we now know as his letter to the Philippians. It was here, from prison, that Paul wrote of a secret that he had discovered and that he was able to maintain when on top of the world, like the writer of Ecclesiastes and Markus Persson, *and* when living at the bottom of the barrel from the cold, harsh confines of an inhospitable jail cell:

I have learned in whatever situation I am to be content. I know how to be brought low, and I know
how to abound. In any and every circumstance, I
have learned the secret of facing plenty and hunger,
abundance and need. I can do all things through
him who strengthens me. (Philippians 4:11–13)

This "secret" gave Paul joy in a jail cell. It also gave Isaiah opti-
mism in the face of an anticlimactic and isolating calling. It is a
secret that is, through the ministry of Scripture, the people of God,
and the Holy Spirit, also available to us. And what is this secret? It's a
present, inner poise that comes from knowing that Christ is with us
to the very end (Matthew 28:20), that we are surrounded at all times
by a great cloud of witnesses who have suffered before us (Hebrews
12:1), and that a New City is coming, one where there will be no
more death, mourning, crying, or pain (Revelation 21:1–5).

Both Paul and Isaiah were men who had learned to live in
present strength because of a future *hope*, a hope that Bishop N. T.
Wright described as the God-given ability to "imagine God's future
into the present."[7]

Isaiah, whose job was to exercise leadership in the preaching
of God's Word—only to be despised and rejected—recorded these
words from the Lord:

For as the rain and the snow come down from
heaven
and do not return there but water the earth,

> making it bring forth and sprout,
>   giving seed to the sower and bread to the eater,
> so shall my word be that goes out from my mouth;
>   it shall not return to me empty,
> but it shall accomplish that which I purpose,
>   and shall succeed in the thing for which I sent
>   it. (Isaiah 55:10–11)

Similarly, from the anticlimactic confines of his jail cell, Paul wrote:

> One thing I do: forgetting what lies behind and straining forward to what lies ahead, I press on toward the goal for the prize of the upward call of God in Christ Jesus. (Philippians 3:13–14)

And also:

> For to me to live is Christ, and to die is gain. If I am to live in the flesh, that means fruitful labor for me. Yet which I shall choose I cannot tell.... My desire is to depart and be with Christ, for that is far better. But to remain in the flesh is more necessary on your account. (Philippians 1:21–24)

Did you catch that? Paul and Isaiah both found purpose in work that, to most, would feel like a supreme letdown and failed leadership. Isaiah was rejected and listened to by no one, yet the words he spoke on God's behalf would *accomplish* a supreme purpose. Paul was thrown into jail, yet he regarded his work—even from that musty, oppressive jail cell—as *necessary* work.

Finding purpose and satisfaction and hope in work that appears anticlimactic can seem impossible. In a sense, we are all like Sisyphus, the Greek mythological character, aren't we? Because of his selfish ambition and deceitfulness, Sisyphus was condemned to eternal punishment. His sentence consisted of rolling a large rock to the top of a hill. Each time he got close to the top, the rock would slip out of his grasp and roll back down to the bottom. For the rest of eternity, he would be doomed to repeat this frustrating task.

One time, J. R. R. Tolkien, looking for an outlet for his Sisyphus-like frustration with his own work, penned a short story called "Leaf by Niggle." The story's main character is an artist who has been commissioned to paint a mural on the side of city hall.

Niggle spends his entire career attempting to create the mural about which he dreamed: a large, robust, colorful, and fruit-bearing tree that would inspire many. But in the end, the artist is only able to eke out a single leaf. After this, he dies. On the train to heaven, Niggle sees a vague yet familiar image in the distance. He asks the conductor to stop the train. He steps off the train and, as he approaches the object, discovers that it is a tree—*his* tree—complete and more lovely and fruitful than he ever hoped or imagined. And there, right in the middle of the tree, is his contribution—Niggle's leaf for the whole world to see.

It is then that Niggle realizes that his little leaf is a part of something grand, a part of a Greater Work by a Greater Artist for the enjoyment and flourishing of a Greater and Everlasting City.

I'm told that Tolkien wrote "Leaf by Niggle" as a way of processing his feelings of anticlimax about another work that he had spent years of his life creating. He was convinced that this painstaking project would never be seen, enjoyed, or appreciated by anyone.

The name of this presumably insignificant work was *Lord of the Rings*.

Tolkien's own story, and the short story that proceeded from it, compels us to again consider Paul and Isaiah. In his first letter to the Corinthians, Paul quoted the prophet Isaiah, saying, "No eye has seen, nor ear heard, nor the heart of man imagined, what God has prepared for those who love him" (1 Corinthians 2:9).

Paul, the New Testament leader who knew anticlimax, found strength from Isaiah, the Old Testament leader who had known anticlimax too. This same Isaiah would later become the most quoted prophet in the New Testament, and his once-rejected words would become the chief source material for the lyrics of Handel's *Messiah*, one of history's most celebrated musical masterpieces.

Are you a leader whose dreams have been spoiled or even shattered? Have you tasted the anticlimax experienced not only by Markus Persson and Peter from *Office Space* but also by biblical writers like the author of Ecclesiastes and Isaiah and Paul … and even Jesus himself?

In those moments when you are tempted to *stop* pressing on and to give up, I encourage you to visit, and then revisit, the story of "Leaf by Niggle." I encourage you to consider not only the past but also the future, where the significance of *your* life's work, which may seem like only a leaf or two, will be revealed as an essential part of the tree that God will place right in the middle of *his* City—the great Tree of Life, which will be for the healing of the nations (Revelation 22:2).

Although it is sometimes hard to believe that your work, done for God's glory, has enduring significance, it absolutely does. Tim Keller and Katherine Alsdorf do a tremendous job of explaining the significance of Niggle's leaf and how it relates to our present stories:

> There really is a tree. Whatever you are seeking in your work—the city of justice and peace, the world of brilliance and beauty, the story, the order, the healing, it is there. There is a God, there is a future healed world that He will bring about and your work is showing it (in part) to others. Your work will only be partially successful on your best days, in bringing that world about. But inevitably, that whole tree that you see—the beauty, the harmony, justice, comfort, joy and community—will come to fruition. If you know all this, you will not be despondent that you can only get a leaf or two out of this life. You will work with satisfaction and joy.[8]

These comments help me see that my work, whether I recognize it or not—whether anyone else recognizes it or not—fits into God's overarching plan.

What you are doing matters.

Don't ever forget that.

"You have heard that it was said, 'You shall love your neighbor and hate your enemy.' But I say to you, love your enemies and pray for those who persecute you, so that you may be sons of your Father who is in heaven."

Matthew 5:43–45

Chapter 7

Opposition: The Unlikely Pathway to Neighbor Love

As I write this, I am keenly aware that the "United" States are more *divided* than ever. It seems that our so-called melting pot of diversity, where "All men are created equal," has largely become a culture of suspicion, division, fear, and crippling violence. Terror and hate are no longer news from the other side of the world. Terror and hate have come to our doorstep and have taken up residence here.

Earlier this year for two Sundays in a row, our church made last-minute decisions to change the sermon focus because of tragic events. During the first week, forty-nine people died in a massacre that took place in Orlando, Florida. A man, claiming jihadist motivations, entered a gay nightclub and opened fire with an assault weapon. The following week, the violence continued when several race-related killings took place. An unarmed black man was shot dead, then another black man, then a police officer, then several more police officers, and then another black man. All over the United States, and for good reason, people have begun to wonder if death and violence are the new norm.

This escalating culture of violence and death is a by-product of subtler hostilities that lie beneath the surface in human hearts everywhere. A quick glance at the news or the average social media feed reveals an undercurrent of hostility. Hatred and anger can be seen in many spheres, including the most polarizing, bizarre presidential election cycle that the United States has ever experienced.

The Republican candidate was a billionaire business tycoon who openly insults women, has a history of supporting the pornography industry, calls his opponents "losers," makes fun of people with disabilities, boasts about his marital affairs and the size of his private parts, admits to never having confessed a sin to God, shows little compassion for war-torn and terrorized refugees, talks flippantly about the "virtues" of torture tactics, and threatens to kill the families of his enemies.

The Democratic candidate considered it her personal mission to make abortion rights more accessible and celebrated than ever. She made public statements that threatened the viability of faith-based institutions that, for reasons of conscience, are unable to embrace the secular vision for sexuality inside their organizations. If her wishes became reality and were codified into law, it could have led to loss of resources, community, and place for many faith groups, including Jewish, Muslim, and Christian organizations. In the name of tolerance, certain historic and biblical views would have no longer been tolerated. In the name of equality, people holding these views would have no longer received equal treatment under the law. According to a friend of mine who is a Washington insider, things would have become "very tough on religious freedom" for faith-based leaders and organizations under her presidency.

In such a climate, Christian leaders must ask several questions: How can we *lead* in a climate that seems increasingly contrary to historic Christian beliefs and that even, in some instances, treats Christian beliefs as evil? How can we promote certain virtues, such as the sanctity of all human life (the unborn *and* those who are disabled, the elderly, the poor, racial minorities, immigrants, and refugees, etc.), when those in power, regardless of their party, have explicit agendas to *diminish* the dignity and flourishing of certain forms of human life? How can we be faithful, cooperative, life-giving citizens of earthly kingdoms when those same earthly kingdoms threaten and even promise to punish the very virtues that good citizenship requires?

To these and all related questions, the answers from Scripture are clear: *Do not fear*; God is with you. *Do not hate*; your true enemy is not visible, but invisible.

It is remarkable to me that the most repeated command in the Bible is "Do not fear." Christians in particular should not fear because the final chapter of the Story in which we live has already been written. We are told in Revelation of a New Heaven and a New Earth when the old, hostile, chaotic, divided world in which we now live will pass away and everything will be made new.

The reign of Jesus will be fully and finally established, "and the government shall be upon his shoulder ... Of the increase of *his* government and of peace there will be no end" (Isaiah 9:6–7). Under *his* reign, there will be no more death, mourning, crying, or pain, no suffering or sorrow or disharmony or division, because God will have set his world right again (Isaiah 9:6–7; Revelation 21:1–8). Lambs will be at peace with lions, snakes with scorpions, and (yes, it's true) liberals with conservatives. All nations and cultures and colors will live as one, and power—all power—will be used *only* to love and to serve and *never* to coerce, subdue, control, shame, punish, or destroy.

If you are a Christian leader, boss, or influencer, a time may come when your faith is costly to you and also to those whom you lead and serve. A time may come when certain organizations are put out of business because faithful Christianity becomes incompatible with the dogma, moral vision, and laws of the land. A time may come when religious freedom gives way to religious persecution for those who stand firm in their commitment to be disciples of Jesus versus disciples of prevailing culture. Perhaps what was true of Christians in ancient Rome, and what is *still* true of Christians in other parts of the world today, will also someday become true of us—losing our livelihoods, our friends, our families, and even our own lives for Jesus's sake.

Even if these things do occur in our lifetimes, it should not come as a surprise to us because Jesus said that, in this world, we will have trouble and that people will hate his followers because of him. Jesus said that those who remain loyal to him will be persecuted and have false things said about them. He said that if we want to be his followers, we will have to deny ourselves daily, take up a cross, and follow him. The apostle Paul similarly said, "It has been granted to you that for the sake of Christ you should not only believe in him but also suffer for his sake" (Philippians 1:29). And he also said that he wanted to "know [Christ] and the power of his resurrection, *and* may share his sufferings, becoming like him in his death" (Philippians 3:10).

If things get worse for Christians in the United States— much worse than they are now—we should not be undone or obsessed about reclaiming "the good old days," as if the good old days ever really existed. Rather, the Bible's encouragement *not* to fear stands true especially in a climate of opposition and persecution. Jesus is with us and is for us in any and every circumstance. If Paul can declare from a Roman prison cell that, through Christ, he was able to be content in every situation, whether facing plenty and abundance, hunger or need, then we can certainly, and in any circumstance, declare the same. Our hope is not anchored in this present world but in the world to come. Because this is true, our long-term *worst*-case scenario is resurrection and everlasting life, an eternity of perpetual and unending strength, momentum, and bliss. The wind will forever be at our backs. It will be a world in which, as C. S. Lewis has said, every day will be better than the day before. It will also be a world in which, as J. R. R. Tolkien has said, everything sad will come untrue—sorrow will be no more, and all things will be redeemed.

So lead on, Christian influencer. Even if things get so bad that you are tempted to throw in the towel, even if your every effort to love, lead, and faithfully serve your neighbors gets squashed, even if the world responds to your love with rejection and resistance, you must continue to love on and to lead on. Even if the world starts feeling to you like a sinking ship, there is good reason to find a piece of brass on the *Titanic* to start polishing. For the task of Christian leaders is to remind themselves—and also those whom they lead—that neither death nor mourning nor crying nor pain nor opposition nor hostility nor persecution nor anything else gets to dictate the story line in the Story of God, the last chapter of which has been written and published and has firmly solidified history's future.

Pause for a moment and exhale. Then breathe this in deeply:

> If God is for us, who can be against us? He who did not spare his own Son but gave him up for us all, how will he not also with him graciously give us all things? Who shall bring any charge against God's elect? ... Who shall separate us from the love of Christ? Shall tribulation, or distress, or persecution, or famine, or nakedness, or danger, or sword? ...

> No, in all these things we are more than
> conquerors through him who loved us. For I am
> sure that neither death nor life, nor angels nor
> rulers, nor things present nor things to come,
> nor powers, nor height nor depth, nor anything
> else in all creation, will be able to separate us
> from the love of God in Christ Jesus our Lord.
> (Romans 8:31–33, 35, 37–39)

Do we believe this? Even if we struggle to believe it, it is no less true. In the end, *Jesus wins*.

But there's more. If Christian leaders and influencers and organizations do fall on hard times, if we lose favor and become a persecuted minority, it might actually mark the beginning of our truest impact. Any serious reading of Scripture confirms that it is not from a place of worldly or political power and privilege that God's people have through the centuries found their firmest footing. Instead, it's from a place of weakness and disadvantage. Historically, Christians have most influenced society not as some sort of "moral majority" but as a life-giving, love-driven minority. This is why I am inspired by these words from the novelist Madeleine L'Engle:

> We draw people to Christ not by loudly discredit-
> ing what they believe, by telling them how wrong
> they are and how right we are, but by showing
> them a light that is so lovely that they want with
> all their hearts to know the source of it.[1]

Beneath Madeleine L'Engle's words is an unmistakable truth: *no amount of cultural opposition stopped Jesus from working to change the world through love.* Because we are his followers, opposition is our opportunity to walk in the path of the One who loved us and gave himself for us, to resist cynicism and despair and fear. We can channel our efforts toward lives of radical kindness, generosity, and love for a hurting world, even if a hurting world does not love us back.

Opposition is our opportunity not only to show the world a different kind of friend but also to show the world a different kind of enemy:

> You have heard that it was said, "You shall love your neighbor and hate your enemy." But I say to you, Love your enemies and pray for those who persecute you, so that you may be sons of your Father who is in heaven. For he makes his sun rise on the evil and on the good, and sends rain on the just and on the unjust. (Matthew 5:43–45)

With a good look at the cross, these words from Jesus begin to make sense. Because Jesus loved us when we did not love him and died in our place "while we were still sinners" (Romans 5:8), then offering self-giving love toward those who do *not* share and are even hostile toward our beliefs should be one of our most fundamental, core commitments. The more conservative we are in our belief that every word of Scripture is true, the more liberal we will become in how we love *every* kind of person. To the degree that we understand how loved and forgiven we are, we will be among the least offended and least offensive people in the world. We will also be among the most loving, others-oriented, and life-giving people in the world.

C. S. Lewis said that, as we read history, we will find that those who did the most good for the present world were also the ones who thought the most of the next. Although Christians have made some serious and hurtful missteps along the way, to be heavenly minded is to be *more* earthly good, not less.

For example, Christians have shown groundbreaking leadership in science (Pascal, Copernicus, Newton, Galileo, Koop, Collins), the arts and literature (Rembrandt, Beethoven, Dostoevsky, T. S. Eliot, Tolkien, Fujimura, Cash, Dylan, Bono), the academy (almost all the Ivy League universities were founded by Christians), healthcare (many hospitals and clinics around the globe), mercy and justice (Wilberforce with abolition of the slave trade, Mueller with orphan care, Dr. King with civil rights), and much more.

Contemporary, secular observers are also taking note of how orthodox Christian belief, in its purest form, fosters beautiful lives. One shining example of this comes from *New York Times* writer Nicholas Kristof, an avowed agnostic who has written several times on how Christians are always the first to show up and serve, the last to pack up and leave, and by far the most generous with their money in situations where poverty, natural disaster, or some other horrific event has brought suffering to human communities. Another example is Sam Adams, the openly gay mayor of

Portland, Oregon, who gave great praise to Christian leader Kevin
Palau. Palau and the churches he mobilized partnered with Mayor
Adams to serve Portland's most vulnerable, at-risk, and economi-
cally deprived populations.

As people of faith come under greater pressure to forsake their
most deeply held beliefs about God, the world, and a biblically
based vision for human ethics and flourishing, an opportunity is
put before Christians to *be* the "light so lovely" of which Madeleine
L'Engle wrote.

It may be that love across lines of difference and deep disagreement will be Christians' best opportunity to live as the aroma of
Christ in the world. More and more, we should be asking ourselves,
"What would it look like for us to commit our lives, our families,
and the communities and organizations and churches that we lead
to extend neighbor love to a hurting world even when that same
hurting world views *us* as part of the problem?"

When a man asked Jesus, "Who is my neighbor?" Jesus told
a story about a Samaritan. In those days, a Samaritan would have
been considered a religious, political, and moral enemy to Jesus's
Jewish audience. However, in the parable, the Samaritan becomes
the hero. He notices his enemy, a Jewish man, lying on the side of
the road nearly dead. The Samaritan does not ignore or attack or
steal from him as would have been expected. Instead, the Samaritan
provides food, shelter, healthcare, dignity, and follow-up to the
suffering Jewish man.

Meanwhile, two religious professionals, a priest and a Levite,
pass by on the other side of the road. They do nothing to help

their hurting neighbor. For them, this would have been unsafe. If marauders attacked this man, what would stop them from attacking the priest and Levite also? Best to keep a safe distance.

But the Samaritan, the true neighbor who was labeled by every Jew not as a friend to be trusted but as an enemy to be avoided, risks his life to care for the man. You might say, based on the parable, that the Samaritan loves the Jewish poor better than the Jews love their own poor. Put another way, he loves his enemy even better than his enemies love each other.

In a world where people of faith are sometimes treated as "the enemy" in secular society, are Christian leaders in particular thinking like the Samaritan? If not, we should be. As Jesus said, our chief purpose and mission in life is not to defend and protect our own rights, privileges, and comforts. Rather, our chief purpose and mission is to deny ourselves daily, take up a cross, and follow Jesus—even to the death if called upon to do so—all the while taking every opportunity to surprise our neighbors, especially those who do not believe as we do, with a life-giving, otherworldly love. We must never forget that even in a world that's increasingly hostile toward faith, the more heavenly minded we are, the more earthly good we will be.

But before we declare how "all-in" we are with Jesus and take up a cross daily to follow him, before we declare how sold out we are to his vision for loving a world that may not love us in return, we must also consider that eleven of Jesus's twelve disciples died as martyrs trying to do the same. Quite literally, each of them took up his own cross and followed Jesus, all the way to his death.

The early church understood that a life of love did not guaran-tee their safety. To the contrary, sometimes a life of love threatened their safety.

When the plague came to Rome, many Greco-Roman citizens tossed family members into the streets to avoid catching the plague themselves. Christians responded by going out to the streets and offering hospitality to the dying, contagious Roman men, women, and children. Many of those who were given shelter did *not* believe in Jesus but were loyal to Caesar and therefore considered oppo-nents to Christians. Yet it was the Christians who gave them the gift of love, care, hospitality, the gospel, and an opportunity to die with dignity. Many Christians got sick as they opened their lives and homes in this way, and many also died. Concerning this sac-rificial love, Emperor Julian wrote that Christians took better care of Rome's poor and infirm than Rome did. According to Julian, this was a threat to Rome's sovereignty ... and he was right. By the third century AD, the moral fabric of Rome had been transformed by the ministry of word and deed coming from the life-giving, persecuted minority known as the Christian church.

Rather than heralding to the world what they are *against*, Christians should instead be heralding to the world what they are *for*.

It is especially important for Christian *leaders* to consider how they can lead in such a way that nonbelievers feel compelled to consider Jesus. "So far as it depends on you," Scripture says, "live peaceably with all" (Romans 12:18). Instead of using our platforms and influence to persuade other people of faith to take a moral stand against secular ethics, what if we focused on *embodying* Jesus's Spirit-filled, life-giving ethics beautifully and compellingly?

What if, instead of protesting the moral trajectory of culture, we redirected those energies to the vision the prophet Jeremiah spoke to the Jews who were being held in captivity to a hostile, secular Babylon?

> Thus says the LORD of hosts, the God of Israel, to all the exiles whom I have sent into exile from Jerusalem to Babylon: Build houses and live in them; plant gardens and eat their produce. Take wives and have sons and daughters; take wives for your sons, and give your daughters in marriage, that they may bear sons and daughters; multiply there, and do not decrease. But seek the welfare of the city where I have sent you into exile, and pray to the LORD on its behalf, for in its welfare you will find your welfare. (Jeremiah 29:4–7)

What if, as Tim Keller has been known to say, Christians began to take this "minority in exile" vision so seriously that they dedicated their entire lives to it? What if, because of the quality of life, compassion, and care that began to emerge from these dedicated Christian citizens, government officials could start reducing taxes? What if, because of the love shown by Christians to people who do *not* share their beliefs, non-Christian citizens would grieve if Christian citizens were taken out of their cities?

As history has shown, Christians are at their best when they are *telling* the world about Jesus—his grace, love, forgiveness, generosity, and beauty—while also *showing* the world his character and ethics by embodying them in beautiful, compelling ways. The content of our beliefs is important. Equally important is the way that we express them. We must *show* the world "a light so lovely."

At the beginning of this chapter, I mentioned the horrific massacre that took place recently at a gay nightclub in Orlando. Rather than be silent or keep a safe distance, this was an occasion for Christians to heed, in the strongest terms, Jesus's imperative to *love your neighbor as yourself.* This was not a time for Christian leaders to stand up and preach their views about right and wrong when it comes to sexuality. This was a time for love, for compassion, for tears. This was a time to enter into the sorrow and the loss—and not with answers, but with presence. It was also a time to speak up on behalf of fellow image bearers because silence is *never* an option for Christians when abuse and injustice have been perpetrated. As Dr. King once said, "Injustice anywhere is a threat to justice everywhere."

In relation to a gay nightclub, I don't think Jesus would at all be concerned with sending "mixed messages" about expressions of sexuality that are incongruent with the biblical vision of monogamy, inside marriage, between one man and one woman. No, I do not believe that *this* would be Jesus's focus following such a tragic loss of life.

Instead, I believe that Jesus would show up to that gay nightclub to love the hurting men, women, and children who had been left behind. After all, he welcomed sinners of every kind—religious sinners and irreligious sinners, sexual sinners and pious sinners, bottom-of-the-barrel and holier-than-thou sinners—and ate with them. Without caveats. *This* was how Jesus showed leadership. And he took a lot of criticism for it from pious religious folk. But that didn't stop him from extending love and grace to the world around him.

A day or two after the Orlando shooting, I came across a tweet by an LGBTQ advocate named Tamára Lunardo, which said the following:

> Straight friends,
> especially you Christians,
> please know:
> We hear your silence so loud.

According to Lunardo, most of the lamenting about Orlando seemed to come from everyone *except* those who identify as followers of Jesus. It's as if she were saying, "Hey, you Christians, they are hurting in Orlando. So, then, Christians, where are your tears? Where are your outcries? Where is your compassion? If it's there, let us see it and feel it and experience it. If you have a light, Christians, this is most certainly *not* the time to be hiding it beneath a bushel."

There were certainly exceptions to Lunardo's concern, like a thoughtful essay about weeping and mourning together over lives and loved ones lost from Southern Baptist leader Russell Moore. Additionally, Pastor Matt Chandler tweeted this:

What a horrific act of evil. Christians, your Muslim friends and neighbors woke up this morning wondering how they will be viewed. Love them. Also consider the fear and pain this will have in the LGBT community. Let's be the people of God in this heinous and awful violence.

Yet, to whatever degree that Lunardo's concern *is* valid, Christians, and especially Christian leaders, should take a sober look in the mirror. It would be easy to become defensive—but the loving thing to do is to listen. Sometimes those who do not share our beliefs provide the most helpful observations about how we can, and should, follow Jesus better.

In the spirit of showing leadership by loving deeply across lines of difference, I am struck by the following excerpt from an essay written by a former chaplain at Harvard:

The divide between Christians and atheists is deep … I'm dedicated to bridging that divide—to working with … atheists, Christians, and people of all different beliefs and backgrounds on building a more cooperative world. We have a lot of work to do … My hope is that these tips can help foster better dialogue between Christians and atheists and that, together, we can work to see a world in which people are able to have honest, challenging, and loving conversations across lines of difference.[2]

The former Harvard chaplain's name is Chris Stedman.

Chris is an atheist, and he also identifies as "queer."

Is it possible to disagree with each other on sensitive subjects and still maintain meaningful and even loving friendships with each other? Is it not only possible but *imperative and right* to weep and mourn across such lines … in such a way that the *lines* become transformed into *bridges*?

As an atheist and member of the LGBTQ community, Chris Stedman says that he believes it is possible.

As a follower of Jesus and a leader of others who follow Jesus, I believe that it is not only possible but that it is an essential part of Christian discipleship. It is morally imperative for the people of Jesus to weep with all of our neighbors who weep and mourn.

"Who is my neighbor?" the teacher of the law asked Jesus (Luke 10:29).

Your neighbor, O child of God, is anyone who is *near* and anyone who has a *need*.

This is Jesus … the *same* Jesus who healed ten lepers, even though only one of them would say thank you; the *same* Jesus who made a Samaritan the hero of his story about neighbor love right in the face of the reality that Jews hated Samaritans and Samaritans hated Jews; the *same* Jesus who commended Rahab for providing refuge for Israel's spies, even though she was still, at the time, an active prostitute; the *same* Jesus who went after Peter in love when Peter had denied him three times, *before* Peter ever repented or said that he was sorry; the *same* Jesus who welcomed a prostitute who had come to him straight off the streets to kiss his feet with her prostitute's lips and douse his skin with her prostitute's perfume. Jesus praised her for her expression of love, regardless of how scandalous it may have been to the cultural norms of the day.

In the spirit of neighbor love, Kate Shellnutt from *Christianity Today* posted this response to Orlando on Twitter:

> Looking for churches volunteering
> or offering security for Pride events
> in light of the Orlando massacre.
> #lovethyneighbor

This provocative comment from Shellnutt feels like something Jesus would affirm. What's more, it feels like something Christian leaders everywhere should embrace and use their influence to instill in the hearts and lives of those whom they lead.

Shellnutt's tweet sounds to me like what Chick-fil-A, a Christian owned and operated restaurant, did in response to the Orlando shooting.[3] On the *Sunday after the shooting*, the day of the week that Chick-fil-A is *always closed* so its employees can attend their places of worship and enjoy a Sabbath rest, they decided instead to make gallons of tea and lemonade and to prepare hundreds of their sandwiches. Then they handed out the food and drinks free of charge to people who were donating blood for the LGBTQ shooting victims.

This is the same company that, because of its president/CEO's belief in the Bible and the historic Judeo-Christian sex ethic, was boycotted by a gay activist. Dan Cathy, Chick-fil-A's president/CEO then reached out *and ended up becoming friends with* the same gay activist.[4]

The truest disciples of Jesus, not in spite of their Christian beliefs, but *because* of them, take initiative to love, listen to, and serve those who *don't* share their beliefs.

Chick-fil-A's response to Orlando is merely an attempt to mirror the action God has taken toward everyone who believes and the reason why anybody ever believes in the first place ...

It is God's kindness that leads us to repent, not our repentance that leads God to be kind. That is, he causes the rain to fall on both the just and the unjust. He places no conditions on, and erects no borders for, his kindness. Neither should we.

Christian leaders, let's make sure that God's kindness is tasted not only on the pages of Scripture but through our lives and through our loving. Because the more we follow Jesus, the more conservative we are in our belief that every single word of the Bible is right and good and true, the more liberal we will be in the ways that we love.

Jesus said to the adulteress, "I do not condemn you. Now go leave your life of sin" (see John 8:11). Reverse the order of these two sentences—"Leave your life of sin, and then I won't condemn you"—and you lose Christianity. Reverse the order of these two sentences, and you lose Jesus.

This is the faithful response. Yes, *this*—to seek with all of our hearts to love our LGBTQ and other neighbors in ways that they would recognize as love. This response may make us suspect in the eyes of those who are religiously smug and relationally scarred.

This response may lead some to even accuse us of being soft on law because we are so heavy on grace. This response may cause onlookers, especially the more pious ones, to mischaracterize us as "gluttons and drunks" because the aroma of Jesus, who was similarly accused, seeps out of us.

In theory this sounds reasonable, but in real life it is messy. As Dostoevsky wrote in *The Brothers Karamazov*, love in practice is a dreadful thing compared to the love in dreams. But real and messy love—the kind that leads us to maintain conviction while communicating love and compassion and empathy to those who might not agree with our convictions—is better than the love in dreams, which is a sentimental love that has no roots. The real and messy love, not the love in dreams, is the love that Jesus entered into. And we must follow.

And so I ask again, is it possible to profoundly disagree with people and love them deeply at the same time? Is it possible to hold deep convictions and simultaneously embrace people who reject your deep convictions?

Yes, it is.

Do you remember Jesus's encounter with the rich young man (Mark 10:17–27), and how Jesus told the man to sell all of his possessions, give to the poor, and then follow him? The young man turned away from Jesus because he had great wealth. If you do remember the encounter, did you catch these two incredibly significant details?

First, Jesus looked at the man *and loved him.*

Second, the man walked away from Jesus *feeling sad.*

The man did not walk away from Jesus ticked off or feeling judged. He did not feel bullied or dismissed or excluded or marginalized. He did not say to Jesus and his followers, "I hear your silence so loud." No. Not these things. But *sad*. The man walked away in the tension of paradox—held captive by the chains of his money idol, yet sensing the loss of a different and perhaps more life-giving form of wealth.

So then, in our secularizing culture, let's again ask ourselves what will matter more to us in the end—that we successfully put others in their place, that we proudly took a "moral stand" regardless of who we alienated and whose fragile spirits we crushed in the process? Or will it be more important that we loved so well that lines and barriers were turned into bridges?

God have mercy on us if we do not love well because all that matters to us is being right and winning culture wars and taking moral stands that put people in their place but don't win any people's hearts. Truth and love can go together. Truth and love *must* go together.

Peter wrote these words in a climate in which Christians were routinely made fun of, maligned, and persecuted for their convictions:

> In your hearts honor Christ the Lord as holy, always being prepared to make a defense to anyone who asks you for a reason for the hope that is in you; *yet do it with gentleness and respect*, having a good conscience, so that, when you are

slandered, those who revile your good behavior
in Christ may be put to shame. (1 Peter 3:15–16)

Critics turned to friends, lines turned to bridges—*through gentleness and respect.* Instead of passing judgment, listen to the cries and sorrows. Instead of "walking by on the other side of the road," show compassion toward *all* of our neighbors in need, whether they believe as we do or not. Whatever our sphere of influence, this is the essence of true servant leadership.

And then, to whatever degree that this approach—the *Jesus* approach—is met with opposition, take to heart these words that Mother Teresa kept on her wall as she fought for Calcutta's poor:

> Give the world the best you have, and it may
> never be enough.
> Give the best you've got anyway.

"We rejoice in our sufferings, knowing that suffering produces endurance, and endurance produces character, and character produces hope, and hope does not put us to shame, because God's love has been poured into our hearts through the Holy Spirit who has been given to us."

Romans 5:3–5

Chapter 8

Suffering: Leading with a Limp

The past year has been a hard one for me personally. It's also been hard for the community that I am part of.[1]

With my dear mom, we are in the later stages of what those familiar with Alzheimer's call "the long good-bye." Dad, who has been nothing short of stellar in the way he has cared for Mom, has also buried his own mom, had two major surgeries, and, now in his midseventies, is flat-out tired.

In our Nashville and Christ Presbyterian community, there are cancers and Lou Gehrig's disease and dementia and funerals, many of which feel woefully premature. Since our community's inception, fifteen sets of parents have buried their own children and reluctantly released their boys and girls into the everlasting arms of Jesus. The most recent was a middle school boy with his whole life ahead of him. He was a talented musician, an exceptional runner, a state champion gymnast, and a jokester who brought levity to every gathering he was part of. And, most lovely of all, this boy had a deep, authentic faith in the Lord.

Earlier this week, a Nashville news anchor and member of our church conducted an interview with the beloved Ben Ellis, a high school teacher in our community who has been afflicted with terminal cancer. Ben—whose leadership has more to do with his character than it does with position, power, or fame—might be the kindest schoolteacher our daughters have ever encountered, and they are not alone in feeling this way about him.

Ben's interview was related to a video that went viral after Tim McGraw, a well-known Nashville musician, posted a video of over four hundred high school students from Christ Presbyterian Academy worshipping God outside of Ben's bedroom window. Recognizing that worshipping God with others is one of Ben's favorite things to do, the school administrators and teachers decided that it was more important to show love to Ben and his family than to continue with the day's class schedule. This community is remarkable in its impulse and capacity for love and compassion. To experience sickness, sorrow, pain, or death here is to also taste the love of God as expressed through people who are tethered to Jesus, the Servant who suffered.

A day or two after the video reached over twenty million views and national news outlets began reporting about it, Russ Ramsey, the Ellises' friend and former pastor, stopped in for a visit. In their brief conversation, Ben relayed to Russ that he had been praying God would give him a few more days, to create more opportunity for the message of God's grace and love to be told to more people through his affliction.

Can you imagine praying for more time *for that purpose?* Can you imagine praying that over praying for healing or release from suffering? But that's where a heart filled with passion for the Lord's purposes and glory will ultimately be.

Ben Ellis revealed part of the essence of true gospel leadership—*a readiness even to suffer and endure affliction so that others who suffer and are afflicted might find hope.*

Yet sickness, sorrow, pain, and death are still horrible things. They are an assault on human dignity, human community, and human flourishing. What are we to do with it when it comes to us? In Ben Ellis's case, suffering became an occasion for him to lead and love. For those in tune with the Holy Spirit, even suffering and death can become a gateway to a place of authenticity, healing, and hope.

Leading with Lament and Protest

Once, while ministering in a worship service at a maximum-security jail, I observed guest musicians from a comfortable suburb take the stage to lead the prisoners in a worship song. Many of the prisoners were serving life sentences and would never again spend a night in a room that was not behind bars. Ironically, the lyrics of the song included the words "Jesus ... in your presence, our problems disappear."

As well-intended as the suburban musicians were in their effort to encourage the prisoners, this lyric was not only dishonest in relation to the prisoners' experience—for their lives were *filled* with problems—it was also terribly unbiblical. For it was Jesus himself who said, to the soon-to-be "leaders" of his Great Commission, that in this world we *will* have trouble, and that, in his presence, the problems encountered by his followers would *not* disappear but would actually increase.

Jesus promised that his followers and those who lead them would be persecuted, have all kinds of evil and false things said about them, and even be put to death ... not *in spite* of their love for Jesus, but *because* of it. He never promised that we would have trouble-free lives here on earth; instead, he said that his followers will take up their cross daily in following him.

Jesus's followers will be afflicted by the same sickness, sorrow, pain, and death that are experienced by the rest of the world. We, too, will experience the horror of miscarriage, broken relationships, a life-altering diagnosis, unemployment, false accusation, personal rejection, and more. And when such horrific things do happen to us, rather than falsely singing about how in God's presence our problems will disappear, the proper response is faith and trust that *includes* lament and protest.

If Jesus could weep and get angry at the tomb of his friend Lazarus (John 11:1–37) and if the apostle Paul could argue with death and mock it as an enemy (1 Corinthians 15:53–57), then certainly God doesn't expect us to shrug and smile at death. Sickness, sorrow, pain, and death were not part of Eden; neither will they be part of the New Heaven and New Earth (Revelation 21:1–5). In other words, these are *not natural* things. They are unwelcome invaders, uninvited guests who have weaseled their ugly selves into the Garden City of God's Delight. And so, like the body rejects a virus by vomiting and fever, so our bodies and souls viscerally reject sickness, sorrow, pain, and death.

Most Bible readers are familiar with the life of Job, the sufferer who was afflicted with sores from head to toe and who was reeling from the grief of burying all ten of his children. It was Job who said, "Though [God] slay me, I will hope in him." What is often left out, however, are the words that immediately follow: "… yet I will argue my ways to [God's] face" (Job 13:15).

There are also the Psalms, which are filled with lament, protest, and complaint. David, a political leader and the man after God's own heart, said, "How long, O LORD? Will you forget me forever?" and "I pour out my complaint before [God]" and "No refuge remains to me; no one cares for my soul" and "My God, my God, why have you forsaken me?" (Psalms 13:1; 142:2, 4; 22:1).

In the end, both Job and David—one a pillar of his community and the other the king of a nation—interpret (and in some ways correct) their feelings on the basis of what they know about the character of God. David, in response to his question to his own soul—"Why so downcast, O my soul?"—preaches to himself, saying, "Put your hope in God, for I will yet praise him." Rather than stuff down their feelings about sickness, sorrow, pain, and

death, both Job and David boldly pray their feelings. They get
their feelings out. They treat their anger and sorrow and tear ducts
as the release valves God created these things to be.

In Job-like and David-like and Jesus-like fashion, there
have been other faithful lamenters/protesters. One is Nicholas
Wolterstorff, a professor at Yale who, having lost his son Eric to
a rock-climbing accident, wrote these words in his heartrending
Lament for a Son:

> How is faith to endure, O God, when you allow all
> this scraping and tearing on us? You have allowed
> rivers of blood to flow, mountains of suffering
> to pile up, sobs to become humanity's song—all
> without lifting a finger that we could see. You
> have allowed bonds of love beyond number to be
> painfully snapped. If you have not abandoned us,
> explain yourself. We strain to hear.[2]

Similarly, the Oxford professor C. S. Lewis prayed his heart-
ache and bewilderment in *A Grief Observed* after losing his wife,
Joy, to a brutal cancer:

> Meanwhile, where is God? ... When you are
> happy, so happy that you have no sense of needing
> Him, so happy that you are tempted to feel His
> claims upon you as an interruption, if you remem-
> ber yourself and turn to Him with gratitude and

praise, you will be—or so it feels—welcomed with open arms. But go to Him when your need is desperate, when all other help is vain, and what do you find? A door slammed in your face, and a sound of bolting and double bolting on the inside. After that, silence. You may as well turn away. The longer you wait, the more emphatic the silence will become ... What can this mean? Why is He so present a commander in our time of prosperity and so very absent a help in time of trouble?[3]

Jesus wept. Jesus got angry.

Jesus repudiated sickness, sorrow, pain, and death. So can we. So *should* we. In a weary, sin- and sorrow-sick world, it's part of how we lead well. Just as Jesus frees us to be hopeful about the renewed world that is to come, he frees us to be realistic about the fallen world in which we now live.

Wounds That Can Make Us Healers

While Jesus invites us to join him in honest protest and lament over brokenness and pain, he also invites us into redemption and hope. In my book *Befriend*, I wrote candidly about my seasons of struggle with anxiety and depression. One season flattened me physically, spiritually, and emotionally to the point where, though not suicidal, I prayed daily that God would either heal the affliction or end my life. I could not sleep despite taking sleeping pills, lost thirty pounds, and could barely eat or get out of bed. If you had quoted Romans 8:28 to me or referenced other Scripture promising that God would work my situation out for good, it would have fallen on deaf ears.

In retrospect, however, I can now see the hand of God in that horrid season.

Two years into my role as senior pastor of Christ Presbyterian, I shared the story of my anxiety and depression with our congregation. At the end of the service, a man in our congregation approached me and said, "Scott, I think you are a gifted communicator. But, and please don't take this the wrong way, you need to know that I am entirely unimpressed by that. But today, when you shared with the whole church about your emotional struggle … I want you to know that today you became *my* pastor."

Anne Lamott has said, "It's okay to realize you're crazy and very damaged, because all of the best people are."

Similarly, and from the wheelchair she has been sitting in since she was a teenager, Joni Eareckson Tada said, "Sometimes God allows what he hates to accomplish what he loves."

If anyone has the right to say that kind of thing, it is Joni. God hates her wheelchair even more than she does because it represents an assault on the way he created things to be. But God, most certainly, also *loves* the encouragement and hope that have been brought to millions. Joni's story and work continue to bring hope and help to many with disabilities and/or special needs, as well as inspiring so many others to look for God's redemption in the midst of their own brokenness and pain.

Another picture of God's healing grace is found in Steven Curtis and Mary Beth Chapman, who lost their daughter Maria in an accident in May 2008. The Chapman family continues to deeply feel the loss of Maria and miss her dearly. In response to this heartbreak and in honor of Maria, Steven and Mary Beth have doubled-down on their work with Show Hope, a nonprofit adoption ministry founded by the Chapmans that places orphans with "forever families." Thousands have been touched by Show Hope and experience the ripple effects of the reality of redemption in the midst of brokenness.

There is also Pastor Rick Warren and his wife, Kay, who declared in an honest and raw statement that they "will never be the same" and that "the old Rick and Kay are gone" after losing their son, Matthew, to a tragic suicide triggered by mental illness. The energy of their grief has been poured into helping others who, like Matthew, are afflicted with mental illness. Their most profound response to Matthew's life and death is not despair, but the bold and biblical statement that "broken trees bear fruit."[4]

Elisabeth Kübler-Ross, the grief expert, said that "the most beautiful people ... are the ones who have known defeat, known suffering, known struggle, known loss, and have found their way out of those depths."[5]

Joni Eareckson Tada, the Chapmans, and the Warrens honestly express how they feel shattered, yet they simultaneously *lead* by allowing their scars to point the rest of us toward a healing that comes through suffering.

While it is true that hope can grow from even the deepest wounds, we must be so careful not to tread roughly on hearts rubbed raw from suffering. We don't want to hear anybody insensitively "preach" 2 Corinthians 1 to us in the depths of intense affliction. But the truths of 2 Corinthians 1—that God surely comforts us in times of trouble and allows us to comfort others with the very comfort we have received from him—are what I find myself, secretly and quietly, praying for leaders and others who are in a season of sickness, sorrow, pain, or death. We can show up, be present with them, and pray quietly, resisting the urge to preach to them, remembering the profoundly helpful lyric from Charlie Peacock:

> Heavenly Father … silence the lips of the people
> with all of the answers.
> Gently show them that now is the time for tears.[6]

We don't need to have all the answers. In fact, we shouldn't presume to provide them to people in the midst of grief. We don't need to have the perfect passage of Scripture ready to read or the right hymn ready to sing. We can be present. We can be quiet. And we can grieve with those who grieve.

I pray secretly and quietly that God, in his timing and in his most careful and purposeful way, would gently unfold his plans to prosper and not to harm his children … his plans to give his children—*all* of his children—a hope and a future (Jeremiah 29:11). I pray secretly and quietly that God would work through their afflictions to bring hope to them and into the lives of other sufferers.

A Hope That Promises Everything Sad Will Come Untrue

For my suffering and grieving friends, I also pray that the Holy Spirit would generously give the strength to endure their present sorrows on the basis of what is true about our shared future in Christ.

Every week, as our community at Christ Presbyterian Church prepares to approach the Lord's table, we recite the words, "Christ has died, Christ has risen, Christ will come again." This is the same hope that the apostle Paul, one of the most influential leaders in history, passed on to believers in Corinth. In the fifteenth chapter of his first letter to them, he boldly states that if Christ has not risen bodily from the dead, then Christians are of all people to be most pitied. If Christ has not risen from the dead, then we are without hope and, to quote Shakespeare's despairing Macbeth, we find that "life is a tale told by an idiot, full of sound and fury and signifying nothing."[7]

Yet, as Paul also asserts based on his and over five hundred other eyewitness testimonies, Christ *has* risen. And because Christ *has* risen, we will rise as well. As Steven Curtis wrote in a song about their beloved Maria: "Beauty will rise! Beauty will rise! We will dance upon the ruins, we will see it with our own eyes!"[8]

The once-crucified and abandoned Jesus—who is exceedingly *able* to sympathize with our weaknesses and who submitted to sickness, sorrow, pain, and death *voluntarily*—rose from death. His resurrection assures us that we, too, along with our other friends and loved ones in Christ, will rise in victory over death.

So will the young middle school gymnast to whom we recently said a temporary farewell. Ben Ellis and *his* friends and loved ones will also rise and, like little Maria Chapman, will dance upon the ruins and see it with their own eyes. My mom will no longer be afflicted with the evil that is Alzheimer's; instead, she will be as lucid and witty and kind as ever. C. S. Lewis will be reunited with his dear Joy, and Nicholas Wolterstorff with his dear Eric; for the dead in Christ will rise and live forevermore, all together and before the face of the Risen One himself.

It made my day recently to reflect on this reality with about twenty grandmas and great-grandmas—some of whom are widows and all of whom are aware of their own and each other's mortality. These women grieve deeply, yet they do *not* grieve without hope; for all who are dead in Christ *will rise* (1 Thessalonians 4:13–18).

Sometimes the best, most life-giving way to lead is by suffering well. Sometimes the best, most life-giving way to lead is by refusing to allow death, mourning, crying, or pain to dictate the story line of our lives and of history.

God sees our every tear. Yet he does not merely see our tears; he also *shares* them (John 11:35), and he *stores* them in a sacred bottle as his treasure (Psalm 56:8). God knows what it is like to be separated from a loved one by death, and he knows firsthand the gut-wrenching nature of what it means to bury his boy.

If this does not bring comfort to us today, perhaps it will at some later date. Eventually, we all face death and the fading away of our influence and names on earth. This inescapable reality remains: the mortality rate is still one person per every one person.

Yet this horrible thing called death is not the end … not for God and not for us. All those happily-ever-after fairy tales we have come to love—where Beauty kisses the Beast and the Beast becomes Royalty, where Cinderella gets the glass slipper and marries the handsome Prince, where Little Red Riding Hood is rescued from the lying, deceiving Wolf, and where dragons are cast into the outer darkness, never to frighten and steal, kill and destroy again— these happily-ever-after stories *ring* true because they remind us of the Happily-Ever-After Story that *is* true.

When Christ Presbyterian Academy Headmaster Nate Morrow asked Ben Ellis if there was a message he wanted relayed to the students worshipping God on his front lawn outside his bedroom window, Ellis's response was, "Tell them that it's all true."

Tell them. *It's all true.*

That's leadership. To stare death, sorrow, and anticlimax in the face and anticipate victory. To believe all the way down to our weary and decaying bones that the happily-ever-after stories we always wished were true … are true.

We are now caught, but only temporarily, within the broken, middle chapters of the Story. This Story, though it may carry us through many dangers, toils, and snares, includes a final chapter that has already been written but has yet to be lived. That final chapter is different from the rest, because unlike the earlier chapters, which are temporary, the final chapter is everlasting.

Unlike the earlier chapters, which are filled with tragedy and turmoil and tear-our-guts-out separations, the final chapter is one in which sickness, sorrow, pain, and death will neither be felt nor be feared anymore—because we are bound, we are bound, we are bound …

… for the Promised Land.

The happily-ever-after stories aren't there to help us escape reality. No, not at all. Rather, they are there to help us *re-enter* the Reality that we so easily forget in our frail, fearful condition. The Story that we are living inside of, with its many dangers, toils, and snares along the way, is the Happily-Ever-After Story.

Jesus, our Teacher and Leader, who suffered crushing loss that we might finish as winners through him, has passed on a message through his friend the apostle John. And that message is to *tell them that it's all true.*

My fellow mourners, come and mourn with me awhile. Let's *lead* by weeping and wailing and lamenting and protesting together, and let's do it as far as the curse is found. But let's not do so as those who are without hope. Rather, let's do it as those who know how the Story ends … or, more truthfully said, those who know how the last chapter—the everlasting chapter—*begins*:

> Then I saw a new heaven and a new earth, for the first heaven and the first earth had passed away, and the sea was no more. And I saw the holy city, new Jerusalem, coming down out of heaven from God, prepared as a bride adorned for her husband. And I heard a loud voice from the throne saying, "Behold, the dwelling place of God is with man. He will dwell with them, and

they will be his people, and God himself will be
with them as their God. He will wipe away every
tear from their eyes, and death shall be no more,
neither shall there be mourning, nor crying, nor
pain anymore, for the former things have passed
away."

And he who was seated on the throne said,
"Behold, I am making all things new." Also he
said, "Write this down, for these words are trustworthy and true." And he said to me, "It is done!
I am the Alpha and the Omega, the beginning
and the end. To the thirsty I will give from the
spring of the water of life without payment.
The one who conquers will have this heritage,
and I will be his God and he will be my son."
(Revelation 21:1–7)

When platforms and influence fade and when our time comes,
we can take heart. For C. S. Lewis couldn't have been more truthful
when he said in *The Great Divorce*—and that's what death and sep-
aration feel like, a great and terrible divorce—the following words:

That is what mortals misunderstand. They say of
temporal suffering, "no future bliss can make up
for it, not knowing that Heaven, once attained,
will work backwards and turn even that agony
into a glory."[9]

The rending and rupture of our living nightmares is not the end of the Story; rather, it is the ultimate setup for that day when we will wake up, once and for all and forever, from every living nightmare.

No chilling winds nor poisonous breath
can reach that healthful shore;
Sickness, sorrow, pain and death,
are felt and feared no more.
I am bound, I am bound, I am bound
for the Promised Land.
—Samuel Stennett (1727–1795)

Even when we struggle to believe, these words remain trustworthy and true. In the end our greatest influence may come not from our vision, our preaching, our leading, or our achievements— but through our weakness.

For sometimes the best leaders discover in retrospect that it was their crosses, not their crowns, that contributed most to the healing of the world.

Epilogue

Over the course of my life and ministry, several faithful men and women have been examples to me of the principles laid out in this book. Some I have never met, but I have nonetheless been profoundly influenced by their lives. These include, but are not limited to, the likes of Martyn Lloyd-Jones, William Wilberforce, Eugene Peterson, Martin Luther King Jr., Amy Carmichael, Dallas Willard, Jonathan Edwards, and C. S. Lewis—to name only a few.

Many others I have been able to meet and come to know personally. All are the same in private as they are in public ... and whose private influence on me has been their most profound influence, which says so much about who they are, and especially Whose they are.

One such person is a pastor, author, and leader whom I had the privilege of working alongside for five years—Dr. Timothy Keller. For many, especially in the Christian world, Tim will need no introduction. For anyone who, like me, has long admired Tim from a distance, I thought I would finish this little book with a reprint of a tribute I wrote about him—and shared on my weekly blog—after he announced his retirement from pastoral ministry. I suspect that as you read the following tribute, you will see nearly all of the virtues written about in this book played out. I hope that you will especially appreciate how Tim's life is a picture of private faithfulness as much as it is one of public impact.

My Tribute to Tim Keller
By Scott Sauls, March 6, 2017

A week ago Sunday, my phone started blowing up with messages from friends living in NYC. The occasion was that my friend, former boss, and long-time pastoral and thought mentor, Dr. Timothy Keller of New York City's Redeemer Presbyterian Church, announced his retirement from pastoral ministry effective July 1 of this year. This announcement from Tim is especially significant to me because more than any other person ... and by a landslide ... Tim's influence has shaped me into the pastor, communicator, and leader that I am today.

I first met Tim eleven years ago. I believed it then, and I still believe it now ... that he is the best English-speaking Christian preacher, thinker, and visionary of our time. I am not alone in this. And yet, having also gotten to serve "up close" under his leadership, there are other things about Tim that endear him to me even more than these things. I suppose that now is as good a time as any to tell about them, because that's what you do when one of your mentors announces such a significant transition. So here are a few important things that Tim's example has taught me ...

First, in this weird and troubling age of Christian celebrity where platform building, fame chasing, green room dwelling, and name dropping can easily replace gospel virtues, Tim inspired me with his reluctance to participate in or even flirt with the trappings of Christian celebrity. He never chased the spotlight. He never tried to make a name for himself. The counsel of Jeremiah to his secretary—"Do you seek great things for yourself? Seek them not" (Jeremiah 45:5)—seemed like a life philosophy for Tim as well. Always shy about himself and boastful about Jesus, his ambition was to advance Jesus's kingdom spiritually, socially, and culturally—whether through Redeemer or (notably) through promoting and supporting *other* churches and leaders.

Second, Tim waited until he was almost sixty years old to publish his first trade book. Humbly, he wanted to wait until he was old and wise enough to write the best possible book he could on any given subject. No doubt, his book-writing pace since then has made up for lost time.

Third, in a time of posturing, comparing, and competing—a time when many pastors see each other as obstacles to overcome versus kingdom colaborers to pray for and applaud—Tim has always been the latter. Instead of trying to position Redeemer as New York's Wal-Mart of churches that would swallow up "the competition" with its superior offerings, Tim consistently leveraged time, resources, and energy to build a church planter training organization through which to bring *more* church planters, and with them *more* churches, into the city of New York. He was happy to see other NYC pastors succeed and other NYC churches thrive, even if it meant that Redeemer's "slice of the pie" might become smaller as a result. Tim never had a market-share mentality about Christians in his city, and he *never* targeted members of other churches, either overtly or covertly, so as to lure them to his own church. Instead, he focused on reaching the unreached, paying special attention to the skeptic and the seeker. If someone left Redeemer for another church, rather than getting snippy or defensive about it, Tim would say something like, "Well, that's a good thing. It's going to make _____ Church that much stronger. And that's what we want ... for *all* the churches in New York to be stronger. Redeemer is a *sending* church, after all, and this includes sending some of our best members to other NYC-area churches."

Fourth, even though Redeemer grew and grew (and grew and grew and grew) under his gifted leadership, Tim never embraced the mind-set of "bigger and bigger." Rather, he emphasized quality of ministry over quantity of seats filled (ironically, it is virtually impossible to find a seat at the typical Redeemer service). Early on, his and Kathy's vision was to plant and pastor a small- to medium-sized church in a single neighborhood of Manhattan, with maybe 350 or so people as their community. They never aspired for Redeemer to become a megachurch. Instead, they preferred to be one of many contributors to a broader movement of churches and denominations that would, together, serve their city. Even now, they talk about their hope that the future Redeemer under the leadership of four congregational pastors— David Bisgrove, Abe Cho, John Lin, and Michael Keller—will emerge into a movement that is not mega, but rather a network of numerous, well-contextualized midsize churches that serve New York's many unique neighborhoods. Tim is finishing pastoral ministry with the same mind-set with which he started—not to turn Redeemer into a great church, per se, but rather to participate as contributors to a broader movement to make NYC a great city that resembles the City of God.

Fifth, as Tim's influence grew over the years, so did his dependence on and personal engagement with the hidden, ordinary graces such as daily Scripture reading and prayer. His long-time habit is to pray through Psalms every month and read the entire Bible every year. He also maintains, at age sixty-six, a youthful posture of learning that has him reading about eighty books per year. The prayer that I began praying for myself when I started writing books and serving as pastor of Nashville's Christ Presbyterian Church—"Lord, give me character that is greater than my gifts, and humility that is greater than my influence"—was inspired chiefly by what I saw up close in Tim.

Sixth, Tim and Kathy have a strong marriage. They live their lives together and not separate—face to face in friendship, and side by side in mission ... and that makes such a difference. Rumor has it that they speak Tolkien's elvish language to each other in the privacy of their home (yes, they have some quirks). One of their favorite things to do is read and discuss books together. A little-known fact is that Kathy is equally as smart as Tim, if not smarter. As I understand it, Tim graduated number two in his class at Gordon-Conwell Theological Seminary. The person who graduated number one was Kathy. No wonder their kids are all so intelligent. It is rumored by some that Kathy is the ghostwriter for Tim's sermons (not really, but she could be). And yet, Tim holds his own. The man can write a book faster than most of us can read a book.

Seventh, and as I have previously mentioned in my book *Befriend*, Tim is one of the best examples I have seen of covering shame with the gospel. In five years of serving under his leadership, never once did I see him tear another person down to his or her face, on the Internet, or through gossip. Instead, he seemed to always assume the good in people. Occasionally, he would talk about how having the forgiveness and affirmation of Jesus frees us to "catch people doing good" instead of looking for things to criticize or be offended by. Even when someone had truly done wrong or been in error, Tim would respond with humble restraint and self-reflection instead of venting negativity and criticism. Like the grace of God does, Tim covered people's flaws and sins—including mine on more than one occasion. He did this because that's what grace does … it reminds us that in Jesus we are shielded and protected from the worst things about ourselves. Because Jesus shields *us* like this, we of all people should restore reputations versus destroying reputations, protect a good name versus calling someone a name, shut down gossip versus feeding gossip, and restore broken relationships versus begrudging broken people.

Finally, Tim could receive criticism, most of which came from the outside and was almost always unfair, and it would bring out the best in him rather than bring out the worst in him. By his words and example, he taught me that getting defensive about criticism rarely, if ever, leads to healthy outcomes. He also taught me that our critics, including the ones who mischaracterize and falsely accuse us as pastors, can sometimes be God's instruments to teach and humble us as persons. In Tim's words from one of my favorite essays of his called "How Do You Take Criticism of Your Views?":

> First, you should look to see if there is a kernel of truth in even the most exaggerated and unfair broadsides ... So even if the censure is partly or even largely mistaken, look for what you may indeed have done wrong. Perhaps you simply acted or spoke in a way that was not circumspect. Maybe the critic is partly right for the wrong reasons. Nevertheless, identify your own shortcomings, repent in your own heart before the Lord for what you can, and let that humble you. It will then be possible to learn from the criticism and stay gracious to the critic even if you have to disagree with what he or she has said.
>
> If the criticism comes from someone who doesn't know you at all [and often this is the case on the Internet] it is possible that the criticism is completely unwarranted and profoundly mistaken. I am often pilloried not only for views I do have, but also even more often for views [and motives] that I do not hold at all. When that happens it is

even easier to fall into a smugness and perhaps be
tempted to laugh at how mistaken your critics are.
"Pathetic …" you may be tempted to say. Don't
do it. Even if there is not the slightest kernel of
truth in what the critic says, you should not mock
them in your thoughts. First, remind yourself of
examples of your own mistakes, foolishness, and
cluelessness in the past, times in which you really
got something wrong. Second, pray for the critic,
that he or she grows in grace.[1]

A decade or so ago, I moved with my family to New York
City, thinking I was going to get to serve alongside and learn from
one of the greatest preachers and visionary leaders of our time.
Indeed, I did get to do that, along with a few others. But even
more than this, the man gave me (and us) what McCheyne said is
the most important thing a minister can give to his people—his
own holiness. For me, Tim's life has painted notable pictures of
integrity that exceeds imperfections, character that exceeds gift-
edness, prayerfulness that exceeds pragmatism, other-centeredness
that exceeds personal ambition, generosity that exceeds personal
comfort, and humility that exceeds (even a stellar) impact.

And now, Tim is beginning to paint for us a picture of what
it can look like to finish well. He is providing glimpses of what it
can look like to say with one's life and not merely with one's lips, "I
am, and always have been, unworthy to untie the straps on Jesus's
sandals. He must increase, and I must become less."

And yet, in becoming less, the man is becoming more. For as the man himself has said in sermons, "The less we presume to act like kings, the more like kings we shall be."

Thank you, Tim, for helping me want to be a better pastor, communicator, and leader. Even more than this, thank you for helping me want to be a better man. I know that you're not done running the race just yet, and that there is more to come from you in the training and equipping context. But I'm still going to miss you, sir.

More about Scott Sauls

Scott Sauls serves as senior pastor of Christ Presbyterian Church, a multisite church in Nashville, Tennessee (christpres.org). Scott has been married to Patti for twenty years, and is dad to Abby and Ellie. Prior to Nashville, Scott was a lead and preaching pastor at New York City's Redeemer Presbyterian Church, planted churches in Kansas City and Saint Louis, and taught homiletics (preaching) at Covenant Theological Seminary. Formative experiences have included being an athlete, living in a global city, and suffering through a season of anxiety and depression.

A self-described "accidental author," Scott has released two books prior to this one: *Jesus Outside the Lines: A Way Forward for Those Who Are Tired of Taking Sides* and *Befriend: Create Belonging in an Age of Judgment, Isolation, and Fear*. Influential voices in Scott's life include Tim Keller, C. S. Lewis, Jonathan Edwards, Soong-Chan Rah, Johnny Cash, Joni Eareckson Tada, Paul Tripp,

Ann Voskamp, Martin Luther King Jr., Dorothy Sayers, and N. T. Wright. In his free time you might find Scott relaxing with people or a book, strumming his Gibson guitar, hiking, enjoying live music, or cheering on the Saint Louis Cardinals and North Carolina Tar Heels.

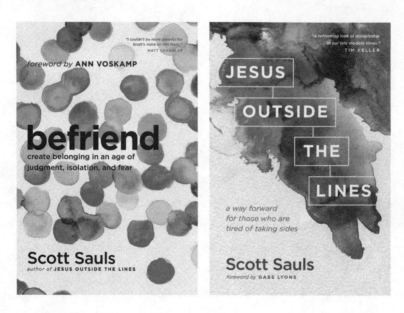

Scott blogs weekly at scottsauls.com.

You can also find him on Twitter and Instagram (@scottsauls) and Facebook (facebook.com/scott.sauls.7).

Scott's sermons are available at christpres.org and at the Christ Presbyterian Church podcast on iTunes.

Notes

Chapter 1: Ambition: The Catastrophe of Success

1. Donald Miller, *Searching for God Knows What* (Nashville: Thomas Nelson, 2004), 116.
2. C. S. Lewis, *The Joyful Christian* (New York: Touchstone, 1996), 138.
3. C. S. Lewis, *The Weight of Glory* (New York: HarperCollins, 2001), 26.
4. Tennessee Williams, "The Catastrophe of Success" (essay, 1947).
5. J. R. R. Tolkien, *The Return of the King* (Boston: Houghton Mifflin, 1994), 930.
6. C. S. Lewis, *The Last Battle* (New York: HarperCollins, 1984), 228.
7. Anne Lamott, *All New People* (New York: Bantam Books, 1989).

Chapter 2: Isolation: The Soil for Collapse

1. John Owen, *The Mortification of Sin* (1656).
2. Pink, "Don't Let Me Get Me," *Missundaztood* © 2001 Arista.
3. Excerpt from the suicide note of Rev. Timothy Brewer, as printed in the *Saint Louis Post-Dispatch*.
4. "How Many Hours Must a Pastor Work?," July 24, 2013, Thom S. Rainer, http://thomrainer.com/2013/07/how-many-hours-must-a-pastor-work-to-satisfy-the-congregation/.
5. Herman Melville, *Moby Dick* (Boston: St. Botolph Society, 1892), 82.

Chapter 3: Criticism: An Invitation to Self-Reflection

1. Rebecca Pippert, *Hope Has Its Reasons* (San Francisco: HarperSanFrancisco, 1991), 93–94.
2. Dietrich Bonhoeffer, *Life Together* (New York: Harper & Row, 1954).
3. Elbert Hubbard (1859–1915), BrainyQuote, www.brainyquote.com/quotes /quotes/e/elberthubb385728.html.
4. Lydia Smith, "Fiftieth Anniversary of Winston Churchill Death," International Business Times, January 24, 2015, www.ibtimes.co.uk/50th-anniversary -winston-churchill-death-memorable-quotes-speeches-facts-about-britains -1484710.
5. Timothy Keller, Twitter, June 16, 2016, https://twitter.com/timkellernyc /status/743444060577345536.
6. The original of this letter first appeared on my blog at scottsauls.com.

Chapter 4: Envy: A Thorn in the Soul

1. C. S. Lewis, *Mere Christianity* (New York: HarperOne, 2001).
2. You can read the full story in 1 Samuel 18:6–16.
3. Tim Phillips, *Bertrand Russell's "The Conquest of Happiness": A Modern-Day Interpretation of a Self-Help Classic* (Oxford: Infinite Ideas, 2010).
4. Stephanie McNeal, "An 18-Year-Old Instagram Star Says Her 'Perfect Life' Was Actually Making Her Miserable," BuzzFeed, November 2, 2015, www.buzzfeed.com/stephaniemcneal/a-teen-instagram-star-is-editing -her-photo-captions-to-show?utm_term=.fxAjJjNyW#.jfQLNLQzP.
5. Mallory Schlossberg, "A Teenage Instagram Star Who Has Modeled for Major Brands Abruptly Decided to Abandon Social Media," Business Insider, November 2, 2015, www.businessinsider.com/teenage-instagram-star -essena-oneill-quits-social-media-2015-11.
6. Karen Yates, "On Christian Celebrities: And How We Are All Broken," blog, October 3, 2013, www.kareneyates.com/2013/10/on-christian-celebrities -and-how-we-are-all-broken.html.
7. Jim Collins, *Good to Great: Why Some Companies Make the Leap and Others Don't* (New York: Random House, 2001), 13.
8. This idea comes from the teaching of Abraham Kuyper.

Chapter 5: Insecurity: Growing Big from Feeling Small

1. U2, "I Still Haven't Found What I'm Looking For," *The Joshua Tree* © 1987 Island Records.

2. Brennan Manning, *The Ragamuffin Gospel* (Sisters, OR: Multnomah Books, 1990).

3. C. S. Lewis, *The Lion, the Witch, and the Wardrobe* (Woodstock, IL: Dramatic, 1989).

4. Lynn Hirshberg, "The Misfit," *Vanity Fair*, April 1991, 167.

5. I first heard this while listening to a sermon by Timothy Keller.

6. Eugene H. Peterson, *Run with the Horses: The Quest for Life at Its Best* (Downers Grove, IL: InterVarsity, 1983).

Chapter 6: Anticlimax: A Gateway to Hope

1. Jacqui Frank and Julie Bort, "Billionaire Minecraft Founder Markus Persson Proves Money Doesn't Buy Happiness," Business Insider, October 6, 2015, www.businessinsider.com/man-who-sold-minecraft-to-microsoft-markus -persson-success-2015-10.

2. Nine Inch Nails, "Hurt," *The Downward Spiral* © 1994 Interscope Records.

3. C. S. Lewis, *The Four Loves* (London: HarperCollins, 1960).

4. *Office Space*, directed by Mike Judge (Los Angeles: Fox, 1999).

5. "What Everyone in the World Wants: A Good Job," Gallup, June 9, 2015, www.gallup.com/businessjournal/183527/everyone-world-wants-good -job.aspx.

6. Paul Sohn, "Why Only 13 Percent of People Love Their Jobs," blog, October 23, 2013, http://paulsohn.org/why-only-13-of-people-love-their-jobs/.

7. N. T. Wright, *Surprised by Hope* (New York: HarperCollins, 2009).

8. Timothy Keller and Katherine Alsdorf, *Every Good Endeavor: Connecting Your Work to God's Work* (New York: Penguin, 2014).

Chapter 7: Opposition: The Unlikely Pathway to Neighbor Love

1. Madeleine L'Engle, *Walking on Water* (Wheaton, IL: Harold Shaw, 1980), 122.

2. Chris Stedman, "Want to Talk to Non-Christians? Six Tips from an Atheist," Q Ideas, accessed October 15, 2014, www.qideas.org/articles/want-to -talk-to-non-christians-six-tips-from-an-atheist/.

3. "Chick-fil-A Opens on Sunday to Give Food to Orlando Blood Donors," WJBF, June 14, 2016, http://wjbf.com/2016/06/14/chick-fil-a-opens-on -sunday-to-donate-food-to-orlando-blood-donors/.

4. Shane L. Windmeyer, "Dan and Me: My Coming Out as a Friend of Dan Cathy and Chick-fil-A," Huffington Post, January 28, 2013, www.huffingtonpost.com/shane-l-windmeyer/dan-cathy-chick-fil-a _b_2564379.html.

Chapter 8: Suffering: Leading with a Limp

1. This chapter's title is taken from the title of Dan Allender's magnificent book, *Leading with a Limp*.

2. Nicholas Wolterstorff, *Lament for a Son* (Grand Rapids, MI: Eerdmans, 1987), 80.

3. C. S. Lewis, *A Grief Observed* (New York: HarperCollins, 2009).

4. Timothy C. Morgan, "Kay Warren: A Year of Grieving Dangerously," *Christianity Today*, March 28, 2014, www.christianitytoday.com/ct /2014/march-web-only/kay-warren-grieving-mental-illness-suicide- saddleback.html.

5. "Elisabeth Kübler-Ross," Goodreads, accessed June 15, 2017, www.goodreads.com/quotes/202404-the-most-beautiful-people -we-have-known-are-those-who.

6. Charlie Peacock, "Now Is the Time for Tears," *Coram Deo* © 1992 Sparrow Records.

7. William Shakespeare, *Macbeth* (1606).

8. Steven Curtis Chapman, "Beauty Will Rise," *Beauty Will Rise* © 1999 Sparrow Records.

9. C. S. Lewis, *The Great Divorce* (London: Geoffrey Bles, 1946).

Epilogue

1. "How Do You Take Criticism of Your Views?," Redeemer, December 16, 2009, www.redeemercitytocity.com/blog/2009/12/16/how-do-you -take-criticism-of-your-views.

PastorServe Book Series

The PastorServe Book Series is dedicated to grace-centered, timeless books for pastors, ministry leaders, and church leadership ministering in a variety of settings in locations around the world. These books expose and address critical issues in pastoral ministry with an emphasis on the relentless love of Jesus. The series focuses on both the front stage and the back stage of pastoral ministry in order to help the reader bring their entire life into alignment with the gospel of Jesus Christ. PastorServe was started by Jimmy and Sally Dodd in 1999 in order that no pastor would walk alone.

Survive or Thrive: Six Relationships Every Pastor Needs

Pastors Are People Too: What They Won't Tell You but You Need to Know

From Weakness to Strength: 8 Vulnerabilities That Can Bring Out the Best in Your Leadership

Watch for more PastorServe titles coming soon!

At David C Cook, we equip the local church around the corner and around the globe to make disciples. Come see how we are working together—go to **www.davidccook.com**. Thank you!

transforming lives together